Jane Suthering, Dip NCHEE, trained at the Birmingham College of Food and Domestic Arts. She spent four years working at the Good Housekeeping Institute and later for other publishing enterprises.

In 1979 Jane went freelance, specializing in food styling for photography and cookery writing. Her books include *Delicious Desserts* and *Step-by-Step Cake Decorating*, and she has been invited to speak a number of times on BBC Radio 4's *Woman's Hour*.

Sue Lousley, BSc, SRD, was until recently Research Nutritionist at the Department of Community Medicine and General Practice, Radcliffe Infirmary, Oxford. In this post and previously as Chief Dietitian at the Radcliffe Infirmary, she worked with Dr Jim Mann in the diabetic unit where the new high-fibre, low-fat diabetic diet was developed. She collaborated with the development of recipes in the bestselling title – *The Diabetics' Diet Book*, also in the Positive Health Guide series.

POSITIVE HEALTH GUIDE

DIABETIC DELIGHTS

Cakes, biscuits and desserts

Jane Suthering
and
Sue Lousley, BSc, SRD

MARTIN DUNITZ

First published in the United Kingdom in 1986 by
Martin Dunitz Ltd, 154 Camden High Street, London NW1 0NE

British Library Cataloguing in Publication Data

Suthering, Jane
Diabetic delights: cakes, biscuits and
desserts.—(Positive health guide)
1. Diabetes—Diet therapy—Recipes
2. Confectionery 3. Desserts
I. Title II. Lousley, Sue III. Series
641.8′6 RC662

ISBN 0-948269-07-3

Phototypeset by Book Ens, Saffron Walden, Essex
Printed in Singapore by Toppan Printing Company (S) Pte Ltd

Front cover photograph shows: *Coconut milk jelly with tropical fruits (top, see page 99); Crispy crunchies and Walnutties (centre left, see pages 56 and 57); Fresh stuffed figs (centre, see page 113); Surprise hazelnut plait (centre right, see page 40); Australian cake (bottom, see page 36)*
Back cover photograph shows: *Cranberry and pineapple shimmer (top right, see page 101); Sunshine bread pudding (bottom left, see page 75); Sarah's summer salad (bottom right, see page 90)*

CONTENTS

INTRODUCTION

People with diabetes know that sugar-containing foods are to them what the apple was to Eve – forbidden fruit. The results of giving way to temptation may not be as drastic for diabetics, but it is generally believed that diabetics should avoid foods with a high sugar content, such as sweets and cakes. The reasons for this are well founded: besides having a high sugar content which can cause hyperglycaemia (see page 14), this type of food also tends to have a high fat and, therefore, a high energy content; that is, it is fattening.

So why are we producing a cookery book specially for people with diabetes that is full of cakes, biscuits and desserts?

We are not suggesting that the situation has altered in any way. Sugar-containing foods should *not* become a regular part of your diet (except those foods that may be substituted into your diet as prescribed by your doctor or dietitian). As this book will demonstrate, it is possible to devise a wide variety of delicious recipes for cakes, biscuits and desserts that do not contain sugar and that can be eaten by diabetics in varying quantities within their calorie- and/or carbohydrate-controlled diet. Indeed many people find it extremely difficult and unpleasant to cut out 'sweet' foods altogether, and there is a very real danger that these diabetics will go to the other extreme and eat exactly what they want. The answer is to find a happy medium for all. Within the confines of your controlled diabetic diet, you can still allow yourself the occasional high-fibre, low-fat 'sweet' food. Knowing this should help you to keep to your diet and enjoy good health and good diabetic control.

A diet that is controlled but varied, and permits the occasional treat is the one most likely to succeed in achieving a balance between healthy and enjoyable eating, as well as being acceptable in the long term.

Controlling your blood glucose levels

Everyone, diabetic or not, needs a balanced diet in order to remain healthy. Diet means the pattern of food and drink you consume, not necessarily food which is advised or not advised for the treatment of an illness. If you have diabetes, you will know that your diet has to be modified to achieve good diabetic control. In other words, to keep your blood glucose (blood sugar) level close to that of non-diabetics, you must be careful about what you eat and drink. To do this, it helps to know about the major nutrients and to be able to recognize the foods you can and cannot eat.

Food – its structure and function

Food is made up of a number of components, all of which are essential for your health. The three major nutrients are carbohydrate, fat and protein and they provide you with energy (measured in kilocalories or kilojoules) and essential raw materials for growth and repair within your body. In addition to these, fibre, vitamins, minerals and water are also essential in the diet to provide bulk and essential chemical elements.

Different foods contain different proportions of these components; for example, butter is nearly all fat whilst milk is made up of fat, protein, carbohydrate and water; milk does not contain fibre, but butter beans contain fat, protein carbohydrate and large quantities of fibre. It is important to eat a variety of foods to obtain a balanced diet. The diagram opposite illustrates examples of common foods containing carbohydrate, protein and fat.

Carbohydrate

There are two forms of carbohydrate in the diet – sugar and starch. Together they form your body's main immediate energy source (as opposed to fat which is your body's main energy store). All carbohydrates are digested and absorbed as glucose, but the rate at which this happens depends on the structure and type of carbohydrate:

Sugar is a very simple carbohydrate which is easily and rapidly broken down and absorbed into the bloodstream. There are various types of sugar, including glucose, sucrose (table sugar), fructose (fruit sugar) and lactose (milk sugar). Sugar is present in large quantities in manufactured foods, such as confectionery, preserves and desserts. Foods, such as potatoes, bread, rice and fruit, contain smaller quantities of simple sugars and larger quantities of starch.

Starch is a more complex carbohydrate; that is, it is made up of many chemical chains of sugar molecules bound together in complicated structures. It takes longer for starch to be absorbed than sugar because it has to be separated and broken down to simple sugar – glucose – before it can be absorbed. The rate of digestion and subsequent rise in blood glucose will vary with the length and conformation of the chemical chains that make up different types of starch.

Fibre

In addition to the physical structure of complex carbohydrate in food, the presence of dietary fibre is a very important factor in

Examples of common foods containing carbohydrate, fat and protein

CARBOHYDRATE **4 kcal/g**	Potatoes, cereals, pasta, plain biscuits, fruit, bread
Carbohydrate and fat	Crisps, fried potatoes, fried bread, shortbread
FAT **9 kcal/g**	Suet, lard, butter, oil, cream, margarine
Fat and protein	Cheese, fried eggs, sardines
PROTEIN **4 kcal/g**	Fish, meat, cottage cheese, boiled and poached egg, poultry
Protein and carbohydrate	Skimmed milk, yoghurt, dried beans and pulses
Carbohydrate, fat and protein	Whole milk, sausages, peanuts

determining the rate of absorption of nutrients in the gut. All food derived from plants contains some fibre, unless it has been highly refined like table sugar. It is now well established that fibre, when mixed with starch, delays the process of digestion and absorption. Generally, the higher the fibre content of a food, the slower the rate of absorption, but this is not always the case. It is now realized that there are two forms of fibre and that the physical nature of the fibre, as well as the quantity, determines the effect fibre has on the rate of digestion and absorption:

Insoluble fibre, found in wheat bran, does not appear to have a significant effect on absorption, although it is important in the prevention of many intestinal disorders, such as constipation, haemorrhoids and diverticular disease.

Soluble or viscous fibre, found in legumes, is far more potent in delaying absorption and reducing blood glucose levels.

The finer details of this process are still not understood fully.

The physical state of food is also directly related to the rate of absorption because cooking alters the fibre composition of food. Raw food is more slowly digested than solid cooked food, which in turn is more slowly digested than puréed cooked food.

So, generally speaking, the refined simple carbohydrates are far more rapidly broken down and absorbed than the unrefined complex carbohydrates, and those with a high soluble fibre content are likely to be absorbed very slowly.

With this information on carbohydrate and fibre, it would be of great benefit to be able to compile a list or league of foods, ranging from foods absorbed at the fastest rate to those absorbed very slowly. This has been attempted in the past in Great Britain by Dr Jenkins who introduced the concept of the glycaemic index. This was based on test meal experiments that measured the effect of 50 g of a variety of carbohydrate foods on blood glucose levels. The simple sugar, glucose, was given a glycaemic index of 100 because it is absorbed very quickly, whereas high-fibre complex carbohydrates, absorbed more slowly, were given a lower index; for example, lentils have a glycaemic index of 29. Although the Jenkins system is a true measure of what happens to blood glucose levels after eating a meal of one food, it does not accurately represent the glycaemic effect of eating mixed meals over a prolonged period. The latter is, of course, the real life situation where many other influences affect the rate of digestion and absorption.

At this stage, the glycaemic index cannot be used to list individual foods in order of preference for day to day eating, although it certainly has its uses in medical research. But it is possible to group foods into those which are high or low in fibre and to divide the high-fibre foods into those that contain soluble fibre and those that contain insoluble fibre (see diagram opposite). As a general rule, you should aim to eat a diet that contains a high percentage of complex carbohydrates to get the beneficial effects that fibre has on delaying absorption and preventing intestinal disorders.

For further details on fibre in the diabetic diet, see *The Diabetics' Diet Book*, another title in this series.

Protein

Proteins are necessary for the production of hormones and antibodies in the body, and for the continuous process of growth and repair of body cells; they are therefore particularly important in children's diets. Excess protein, not needed for these processes, is stored in the body as fat.

Fat

Energy is stored in the body as fat. It is a very concentrated source of energy, providing 9 kcal of energy/g fat – more than twice the amount of energy supplied by a gram of carbohydrate or protein (an important point to remember if you are trying to lose weight). The most obvious sources of fat in the diet are the so-called visible fats – butter, lard, margarine and fat on meat – but there are other important sources of fat that many people forget about, namely, the invisible fats. These include oils, milk, cheese, eggs, lean meat and nuts.

Although fat forms an important part of the structure of the body, and certain fats contain essential vitamins, most fat can be

High-sugar foods	Low-fibre starchy foods	High-fibre starchy foods	
Sugar	White bread	Dried beans eg.	
Meringue	Wheatgerm	butter beans,	
Syrup	White flour	red kidney beans,	
Treacle	Cornflour	soya beans	
Jam	Custard powder	Lentils	**Soluble fibre**
Marmalade	White pastry	Peas	
Honey	White pasta eg.	Fruit	
Lemon curd	spaghetti,	Oats	
Sweets	macaroni	Soya flour	
Chocolates	White polished rice	Oatcakes	**Soluble and insoluble fibre**
Drinking chocolate	Dessert cereals eg.	Muesli	
Ovaltine	semolina, tapioca,	All Bran	
Horlicks	sago	Puffed Wheat	
Bournvita	Cornflakes	Weetabix	
Marzipan	Special K	Wholemeal bread	
Condensed milk	Rice Krispies	Rye bread	
Sugar-coated cereals	Plain biscuits eg.	Wholemeal flour	
Cakes	Cream crackers	Rye flour	**Insoluble fibre**
Sweet biscuits	Water biscuits	Wholemeal pastry	
Instant desserts	Sweet biscuits eg.	Wholegrain pasta	
Sweetened desserts	Rich Tea	Wholegrain rice	
Fruit tinned in syrup	Morning Coffee	Nuts	
Fruit squash		Wholemeal biscuits eg.	
Coca-Cola		crispbreads	
Sweetened fizzy drinks		digestive biscuits	

Different types of carbohydrate in common foods

made by the body from other nutrients, such as protein, when supplies of fat-containing foods are short.

There are three categories of fat in the diet:

Saturated fat – hard, animal fats, such as butter, fat on meat.
Polyunsaturated fat – soft or oily vegetable fats which contain the highest number of essential fatty acids and for this reason are sometimes called essential polyunsaturates.
Monounsaturated fat – such as olive oil.

Cholesterol, which is often put in the same category as the three types of fat, is in fact a fat-like, waxy material, present in the blood and most tissues in the body, especially nervous tissue. Cholesterol is both made in the body and eaten in our diet – for example, in eggs and offal.

Polyunsaturated fat is now regarded as healthier than saturated fat because it helps to lower levels of cholesterol in the blood. This is very significant because high levels of cholesterol in the blood will cause cholesterol to be deposited on the walls of blood vessels thus restricting the passage of blood to the heart. This condition is called coronary heart disease which can cause heart attacks and is the commonest cause of death in all people over thirty-five years of age. Diabetics are particularly at risk from heart disease. Saturated fat tends to increase the levels of cholesterol in the blood and therefore increase the risk of heart disease; polyunsaturated fat helps to reduce the risk of heart disease by lowering levels of cholesterol in the blood. Therefore, in addition to reducing your total fat intake, you should eat polyunsaturated fat in preference to saturated fat which seems to serve no useful purpose in the body apart from providing energy.

For further details about fats and heart disease, I recommend you read *The Healthy Heart Diet Book*, another title in the Positive Health Guide series.

Why do diabetics need to reduce sugar in the diet?

As we have seen, sugar is rapidly absorbed into the blood stream because of its simple chemical structure. Starch, being more complex in structure, is usually absorbed more gradually into the blood. The addition of fibre, especially soluble fibre, will further delay the breakdown of starchy carbohydrates to glucose. This information can be directly related to glucose levels in the blood:

The diagram opposite shows the sharp peaks in blood glucose levels after eating sugar compared to the less extreme and more gradual rise in blood sugar after eating foods which are pre-

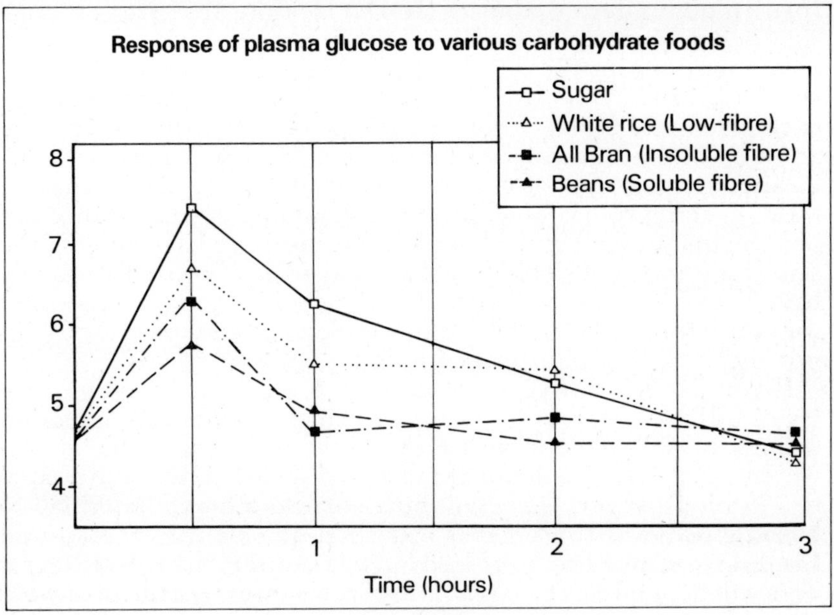

dominantly starch. Therefore, eating too much sugar can completely disrupt diabetic control.

- A rapid rise in blood glucose in a non-diabetic will be counteracted by the immediate release of the hormone, insulin, from the pancreas. Insulin regulates blood glucose at a fairly constant level by helping to remove excess amounts of glucose from the blood to the tissues where it is used to provide energy.
- Insulin regulation is impaired in people with diabetes: some diabetics cannot produce insulin at all, others do not produce enough. Therefore they cannot control blood glucose levels without the help of a specially modified diet and, in most cases, either insulin injections or special tablets.

Your type of diabetes
As you are probably aware, there are two types of diabetes: Insulin dependent diabetes mellitus (IDDM) and non-insulin dependent diabetes mellitus (NIDDM). Although NIDDM in theory should be easier to control than IDDM, a suitable diet including sugar restrictions is important for everyone with diabetes, whether dependent on insulin or not.

Insulin dependent diabetics (IDDs) lack the ability to produce significant amounts of insulin in the pancreas. If you are insulin dependent, an insulin regime and a high-carbohydrate diet will have been prescribed for you and these should counterbalance each other and blend in with your life style. In other words, the amount of insulin you take before a meal will automatically balance the amount of glucose you are likely to eat during the meal, keeping your blood glucose levels stable. A true balance can only be maintained if you have regular meals and eat roughly the same type and quantity of food from day to day. You will probably have been given a carbohydrate exchange list to make this easier for you. This list will include the complex carbohydrate foods but not the concentrated sugary foods.

If you eat a lot of sugar-containing food, your blood glucose levels will rise very rapidly because the insulin from your injection will not be able to cope with such a sudden increase – that is, you will become *hyper*glycaemic (high blood sugar). After such a rapid rise in blood sugar, there will be a correspondingly rapid fall in blood glucose as the sugar is absorbed quickly into the tissues. Insulin is supplied to your body at a fixed rate for a fixed time. This will depend on the type of insulin you use, regardless of what you eat. So if there is a rapid fall in blood glucose, *hypo*glycaemia (low blood sugar) will result because the insulin will continue to act for a fixed time despite blood glucose reaching normal levels. So your blood glucose levels will swing from one extreme to the other before your next meal. A controlled diet, which counterbalances your insulin injections, is very important in the treatment of diabetes.

Non-insulin dependent diabetics (NIDDs) Although your pancreas produces some insulin and your body can cope with a gradual rise in blood glucose, it cannot effectively maintain your blood glucose within its normal range; you may be taking hypoglycaemic tablets to help your pancreas in addition to a special diet. If you eat too much food, particularly concentrated carbohydrates, not only will hyperglycaemia result but you will also put a further strain on your pancreas. Many NIDDs are also overweight and, since sugar-containing food tends to have a high energy content, this is a further reason for avoiding it where possible.

More recently, some studies have suggested that the picture of diabetes may not be that simple. Some research studies in France, the United States and Sweden have suggested that, after meals containing simple sugar, hyperglycaemia and glycosuria (sugar in the urine) are no worse than after meals containing complex carbohydrates. But only a few such studies have been conducted and the majority of them have only looked at the effect of a single meal on blood levels. No one yet knows what would happen if diabetics ate sugar for a long time. In practice, most diabetics regularly consume some foods which contain some sugar, for example, breakfast cereals. It may be that if a large proportion of unrefined carbohydrate is eaten as well as some sugar to ensure a high-fibre intake, this may protect against the effect of the sugar in the diet. However, research into this is at far too early a stage to draw any conclusion at the moment, and sugar must remain a food to avoid.

Although sugar and starch have the most direct effect on diabetic control, the protein and fat content of a diet is also very important. Both protein and, in particular, fat are sources of energy, so if you eat more than your body requires you will put on weight. It is now well known that being overweight causes a deterioration in diabetic control and puts you at high risk from heart disease (see page 12). If you are overweight and then lose weight, your blood glucose levels can improve significantly. Many overweight diabetics who are taking oral hypoglycaemic tablets to achieve good diabetic control could in fact achieve the same results by diet alone if they lost weight. In addition, neither fat nor protein contains fibre and thus foods which have a high protein or fat content will equally have a low-fibre content. As we have seen, fibre is increasingly being recognized as essential for a healthy diet and has clearly been shown to help keep blood glucose levels down in people with diabetes.

To control your blood glucose levels, you should:

- Avoid becoming overweight, or lose weight if you are already overweight.
- Avoid simple sugar.
- Eat plenty of unrefined, high-fibre carbohydrate food – though go steady if you are overweight because all food is fattening if you eat too much of it.
- Eat moderate amounts of protein food.
- Carefully watch the amount of fat you eat, particularly saturated fat, as not only does it have a high energy content but also a high risk association with heart disease. Eat essential polyunsaturated fat in moderation.

How much sugary food can you eat?

This is the sixty-four thousand dollar question! Although there is no hard and fast rule, there are certain general guidelines which should be of some help; for example, exercise will affect the amount of sugar you can, and should, eat.

Being diabetic does not mean that you have to omit all foods containing sugar from your diet. This would not only be extremely difficult to do but, in point of fact, it would not be of great benefit either. Many foods contain some sugar (even bread, for example) but, if eaten in reasonable quantities, they should not upset your diabetic control unless they are very concentrated sources. This is especially true if they also contain a fairly high percentage of fibre, for example, All Bran and other wholegrain cereals, wholegrain biscuits, fruit and even baked beans. The actual quantity of these various foods that can be eaten without ill effect depends on the individual. As people differ in almost every other aspect of their make-up, so they differ in terms of their reaction to diet. People seem to vary in their sensitivity to sugar; for example, some individuals can eat four oranges or more a day quite happily while others find that even one upsets their control. This is equally true of other foods, such as biscuits and cereals. If you test your urine/blood regularly you will soon find out if you are overdoing things. A controlled diet fitted to your individual requirements should control your weight as well. But if you have a tendency to put on weight, exercise and general activity will undoubtedly help to keep your diabetes under control.

Exercise

Regular exercise is extremely good for you; it keeps you fit and improves diabetic control by increasing the efficiency of insulin action. Exercise facilitates the entry of glucose into the body cells thereby helping to remove excessive glucose from the blood. If you are fit and active, you will need a higher energy intake than someone who leads a sedentary life.

Exercise for NIDDs If you are non-insulin dependent and are not taking oral hypoglycaemic tablets, taking exercise simply enables you either to eat more or to lose weight.

Exercise for IDDs If you are insulin dependent and/or are taking oral hypoglycaemic agents, the situation is not as simple. For everyday activities, like shopping, walking or riding a bike to work, your diet will have been planned to provide for your needs. However, for more strenuous exercise, such as spring cleaning or a round of golf, where extra glucose is needed to provide the necessary energy, your normal diet will not be adequate. You will need to supplement your diet with complex carbohydrate foods. The amount of extra carbohydrate needed varies from person to person but, normally, 20–30 g carbohydrate before starting your exercise should be sufficient. You can alter this amount as you become used to your own requirements, which in turn will vary depending on the type of exercise you are taking.

Prolonged activity for IDDs and those taking oral hypoglycaemic tablets If you are taking exercise over a prolonged period, you should eat extra carbohydrate before you start. For example, if you are digging the garden, going for a long vigorous walk or doing exercises, you should eat high-carbohydrate food, such as a sandwich or an apple and a biscuit, as an extra snack before starting. The carbohydrate snack which, as we have seen, should contain starch, smaller amounts of sugar, and plenty of fibre, will sustain you over a prolonged period because the glucose from the carbohydrate will be released slowly. It is important to remember that you should not take extra energy in the form of concentrated sugar for prolonged exercise because you require a long-lasting energy source, not a sudden burst of energy. If the prolonged work is extremely strenuous, you may need to take an extra carbohydrate snack after exercise to prevent hypoglycaemia (see page 14).

Strenuous exercise for IDDs and those taking hypoglycaemic tablets Extremely active sports, such as badminton, squash and judo, require a great deal of energy expenditure over a relatively short period of time. This type of exercise uses up glucose in your body extremely rapidly and the only way to supply glucose at the same rate is to eat simple sugars as a significant part of your extra carbohydrate snack before exercise. In these circumstances, a bar of chocolate, chocolate biscuits, a glass of lemonade or a glucose drink, or similar foods made with sugar (not sweeteners) may be suitable. They will not cause high blood glucose levels because, once the sugar is broken down to glucose, it is immediately transported to the muscle cells to provide energy.

Illness

The only other time that you are likely to need to eat concentrated sugar-containing food is when you are ill and have lost your appetite. In these circumstances, you are still taking either your tablets or your insulin (in fact insulin requirements are often increased during illness) so you still need to eat carbohydrate to balance this insulin. If you are too ill to eat solid food, or your appetite is very poor, it is best to drink small quantities of sugary food regularly (every 20 minutes or so) throughout the day. You should not worry about consuming the correct quantity of carbohydrates as long as the quantity is regular and small. This will prevent hypoglycaemia.

Exercise and illness are special circumstances when a quick release of energy in the form of simple sugars is essential. But in your normal daily life, simple sugars must be avoided and this can prove limiting. Although we have established that it is acceptable to eat foods containing some sugar (a general rule is that if sugar or glucose is not in the first three foods on the list of ingredients, the food is acceptable), this is never the same as being able to eat the very sweet tasting foods, such as cakes and puddings that help to add a little sweet variety to what can become a rather monotonous savoury diet. One obvious solution to this problem is to find sweet alternatives to sugar.

Sweet alternatives

There are a variety of ways of sweetening food without actually using table sugar (sucrose). Sweetening agents are available in their natural form or as commercially prepared products.

Natural alternatives

All dried fruit and some fresh fruit and fruit juice impart a sweet flavour that is distinct and pleasant, and derived from the sugar in fruit called fructose. Fructose is also available in powder form as an artificial bulk sweetener (see page 21). Unlike refined sugar, fruit has the advantage of providing vitamins, minerals, and fibre with all its associated benefits (see page 8). But it must be remembered that because all forms of fruit contain sugar, albeit natural and unrefined, they do have to be counted as part of your daily carbohydrate or calorie allowance. This is also true of honey which can be used in very small amounts as a sweetener in cooking. Fruit sugar and honey have therefore been included in recipe analyses when they have been used in the recipe.

Dried fruit and mashed fresh fruit are excellent for sweetening cakes and teabreads, whilst small quantities of fruit juice can be used to sweeten desserts. When it is not suitable or practical to use fruit, artificial sweeteners can be used.

Artificial sweeteners

There are two forms of artificial sweetener now available which can be used as a substitute for sugar:

- Intense, or non-nutritive sweeteners
- Less concentrated, bulk sweeteners.

The type that you use is determined largely by what you are sweetening, but it is important to stress here that *you should use intense sweeteners in preference, wherever possible.*

Intense sweeteners

These occur both naturally and as chemically produced sweetening agents. They are so concentrated and impart such a sweet flavour that only a minute quantity is required to sweeten food satisfactorily. Thus they are effectively calorie- and carbohydrate-free and contribute nothing to your diet apart from a sweet taste (hence the term, non-nutritive). They are suitable for all diabetics, regardless of the type of diet you are on.

In Britain there are four types of intense sweeteners on the market: Aspartame (Nutrasweet), Saccharin, Thaumatin, and Acesulfame potassium (Acesulfame K, Sweetex Plus or Diamin):

Aspartame is a chemically produced sweetener that is a protein. It is used in the body like other proteins you eat and similarly, it provides 4 kcal of energy/g protein. It does not tolerate heat well. Since it is about 200 times sweeter than sugar, you only need to use very small amounts to sweeten food and drink. It is available in tablet and powder form: one tablet contains less than 1 kcal of energy and a negligible amount of carbohydrate; the powdered form, called Canderel, contains lactose and dextrose as bulking agents which make it slightly less concentrated. Consequently more powder has to be used to provide the equivalent sweetness. One sachet of Canderel provides approximately 4 kcal of energy and 1 g carbohydrate. The tablet form can be used freely, but Canderel should be used more carefully because of its calorie and carbohydrate content.

Thaumatin is an extract of a fruit found in West Africa. It is a protein, almost 2,000 times sweeter than sugar. It is mainly used as a flavour enhancer, although it is becoming more widely used as a sweetener.

Acesulfame potassium is a chemical that is almost 200 times sweeter than sugar. It is available in tablet form and powder form (Diamin). Unlike Aspartame, it tolerates heat well.

Saccharin has been available for many years in tablet and liquid form, and is over 500 times sweeter than sugar. It is now available in powdered form as well, achieved by mixing it with small quantities of a bulking agent. As a result, the powdered forms are slightly less concentrated and contain some calories so they should be used in moderation. The powdered forms of saccharin are:

- **Sweet 'n' Low** – a mixture of saccharin and lactose, available in sachets or a packet. One sachet is as sweet as two teaspoonfuls of sugar but contains only 3.5 kcal (compared to 40 kcal in sugar) and 1 g carbohydrate.
- **Hermesetas Sprinkle Sweet** – a mixture of saccharin and maltodextrin. One teaspoonful can replace one teaspoonful of sugar but provides less than 2 kcal compared to 20 kcal of sugar.
- **Sugar Twin** – again a saccharin and maltodextrin mix. As sweet as sugar but provides less than 2 kcal per teaspoonful.

These powders are useful for sprinkling on food, but they have a limited use in cooking because, like the other intense sweeteners, they cannot be used in large enough quantities to provide bulk. This characteristic is in fact the main drawback of the intense sweeteners. Being so concentrated that they can only be used in small quantities, they provide sweetness but not volume. Sugar is used in cooking not only to sweeten but also to act as a bulking agent to give structure to cakes, meringues, preserves and so on.

When this quality is needed, a different type of sweetener is necessary.

Bulk sweeteners

These can be used to provide both sweetness and volume. The two most commonly available types are fructose and sorbitol. Their use should be limited to those recipes where sugar would normally be used to provide bulk as well as sweetness. They should never be used neat, for example, to sweeten drinks. The British Diabetic Medical Advisory Committee now recommends that a *maximum* of 25 g/1 oz of one or a combination of these sweeteners should be used per day. You should remember that this not only relates to home cooking, but also to bulk sweeteners used in commercial products. There are some important reasons for restricting your intake of bulk sweeteners:

- They all contain carbohydrate and their energy content is very similar to that of sugar. If you are on a weight-reducing diet, you should not use them except perhaps on special occasions. If you are not overweight, you should still remember that bulk sweeteners contain the same quantity of calories as sugar. As long as you do not exceed the BDA recommendations (see above), you do not have to include their carbohydrate content in your daily allowance. In recipes containing fructose, their analysis includes the calorie content but not carbohydrate content, and this is in keeping with the recipe books produced by the BDA (with the exception of their book on preserves where the recipes contain larger quantities of fructose).
- All bulk sweeteners have a laxative effect and can cause diarrhoea if eaten in large quantities. Individuals vary in their sensitivity but it is certainly wise to keep within the limits recommended by the BDA.
- Bulk sweeteners can sometimes adversely affect diabetic control even though they are generally considered suitable for diabetics. Normally fructose and sorbitol are broken down in the liver by a mechanism independent of insulin, and for this reason, fructose and sorbitol are considered to be better than sugar for people with diabetes. But if there is an insulin deficiency in the body, for example, in untreated or poorly controlled diabetes, there can be a highly significant conversion of these bulk sweeteners to glucose which obviously results in raised blood glucose levels and a further deterioration of diabetic control. It is therefore important that you do not use bulk sweeteners if your control is poor or even if you are unsure. For people with good control, the evidence is that they are well tolerated in the quantities recommended by the BDA.

Fructose, also referred to as fruit sugar (brand name, Dietade or Fructofin) is found naturally in a variety of plants, fruits and berries and also in honey (see page 18). It is sweeter than sucrose although the degree of sweetness depends on its preparation and can vary from 15–80 per cent sweeter than sucrose. Generally, if you use approximately one-third less fructose than you would sugar, it will provide sufficient bulk and sweetness. Consequently it is possible to reduce the calories in a recipe slightly since both fructose and sugar (sucrose) provide approximately 4 kcal/g. The drawbacks we already know, and it should be remembered that fructose in its refined, powdered form is similar to sugar because it contains virtually no minerals, no vitamins and no fibre. If eaten in its natural state in fruit, you will get the benefit of all of these.

Sorbitol is a naturally occurring sugar alcohol found in a variety of fruits, vegetables and berries. Like fructose, it is produced commercially in powdered form; unlike fructose, it is only about 50 per cent as sweet as sugar. Since it still provides approximately 4 kcal/g, it follows that recipes using sorbitol are likely to be higher in calories than those using fructose or sugar. Sorbitol is combined with saccharin in commercially produced products, such as Sionon, Sweetex powder and Boots' Diabetic Sweetening Powder. Sionon is as sweet as sugar, and Sweetex powder four times as sweet. Both can be used in baking so they are a useful means of reducing the calorie content.

In summary, fructose and sorbitol should only be used as sugar substitutes in recipes where sugar would normally be used to provide structure as well as sweetness. They can provide much needed variety in cooking and are excellent in preserves, cakes, crumbles and meringues. If you are not overweight and your control is satisfactory, there is no reason why you should not use up to 25 g/day per person of either one or a combination of these sweeteners.

Unsuitable sweeteners

There is a further type of sweetener available that is not suitable for people with diabetes because it contains sugar. This type includes Slimcea Sweet 'n' Slim, Sucron, and Boots' Sugar Lite. The number one rule when buying sweeteners is the same as that for buying any commercially prepared food – always read the list of ingredients first. If sugar is among the first two or three ingredients, the product is usually not suitable for diabetics. As so many canned and packed foods contain sugar, excluding any product containing sugar would be impractical, but try to use fresh ingredients whenever possible and be sensible about the food you buy.

Proprietary diabetic foods

A wide variety of foods specially prepared for diabetics is now available, including jams, cakes, biscuits, sweets and drinks. These do not have to form a necessary part of any diabetic diet and, in addition, they tend to be expensive. Fructose and sorbitol are invariably used as sweetening agents in proprietary products, raising their calorie content to a similar, if not greater, level to that of their sugar-containing counterparts. Low-calorie dietary or slimming foods, such as low-sugar jam or low-calorie squash and carbonated drinks, are of considerably more use because they tend to be less expensive, are suitable for all diabetics, and have the positive advantage of being sweet, low in calories and having no effect on diabetic control.

Of course this does not mean that diabetic food should not be bought; from the large number of products now being sold, it is obvious that there *is* a demand for diabetic foods. They are prepacked, convenient, quick and easy, and include foods, such as sweets, that you are unlikely to want to prepare yourself. But their main disadvantage is their expense. Also many people consider that cakes, biscuits, preserves and so on, taste better cooked at home although that is a matter of taste, how good a cook you are, and how good the recipes are!

Diabetic sweets

The selection of diabetic sweets now ranges from bars of chocolate to boiled sweets and chewing gum. The chocolates tend to contain fructose as a sweetener, while pastilles generally are sweetened with sorbitol or a sorbitol–saccharin mix. Chewing gum is sweetened with saccharin or zylitol and mannitol. All these products list their ingredients and the quantity of fructose or sorbitol used, so you can easily calculate how much you can eat and keep within the limits recommended by the BDA (see page 20). Remember to count the number of calories provided by the sugar substitute in each sweet, but not the carbohydrate values. Also remember that sweets are probably the most unnecessary food that we consume. They contain little or no fibre, few vitamins and minerals and are often very high in calories. Many people find them an irresistible temptation and disastrously easy to nibble in between meals – a major cause of weight increase in children and adults, and a contributory factor in tooth decay. Most people are brought up on the adage that sweets are bad for them but they still continue to eat them; likewise, most diabetics know that sweets are very bad for them but many continue to eat both the diabetic and sugared varieties. Incidentally, the occasional ordinary sweet is probably better than a lot of diabetic sweets.

Diabetic children

It is often taken for granted that the majority of people, especially children, like, and often cannot do without, sweet tasting food. This may be the case but it should not be an automatic assumption. You cannot want or miss something that you have not known – and this is not as obvious as it sounds. Parents feeding their children will tend to encourage them to do what they did as children; for example, if they had sugar on cereal, their children will automatically have sugar on cereal. This principle can be applied to so many things – sugar in tea, sugar on fruit, sugar in puddings, sweets after a meal. None of these things is necessary, but it is sometimes assumed that without them the child will not like and therefore will not eat the food. It is far harder to stop children from eating food, such as sugar, that they are used to than to prevent them from eating it in the first place.

A major problem is that *what* you eat and *when* you eat is largely determined by social factors, whether it is a family meal, a social dinner, or a trip to the local chip shop at lunch time. It is not simply determined by your physical needs. As one grows older, it becomes easier (though never easy) to deviate from the norm and to tell other people that you cannot eat something like sugar because you are on a special diet. Indeed for many women, this *is* the norm! But it can be extremely difficult and very upsetting for a child to opt out of going to the shops with friends to buy sweets. Coping with the facts of diabetes is difficult enough, but for many children the diet is far more of a problem than the insulin injections. Undoubtedly, missing the taste of sweet food is part of the problem, but other major factors contribute, such as having to eat set quantities at set times and the dislike, or even fear, of feeling different and apart from other children and not being able to join in with friends. There is no magic answer to this very real problem and all diabetic children must be made aware of the importance of their diet. Meals and snacks cannot be omitted; high-fat and high-sugar foods should be avoided. One of the hardest facts they have to accept is that they cannot simply go out with their friends and buy a whole bar of chocolate or a bag of boiled sweets and eat all of it.

The ideal course of action, therefore, is for parents to bring up their children on unsweetened foods right from the start; sugar is not needed by any child and is of no benefit to anyone, diabetic or not. But we can discard such an unrealistic solution and consider more practical suggestions. We are stuck with the paraphernalia of sweets, cakes, biscuits and puddings – and we like them.

The best we can do is to suggest ways of controlling your child's sugar intake within the home environment. Having accepted this, it is important to give your child foods he or she likes to eat and not to make life too difficult:

- Remove sugar from home cooking. You will find it far easier to make changes in the home environment than outside the home. But there is nothing worse than having a different meal or dish cooked specially for one person. A diabetic diet is a healthy diet so, if one member of the family is diabetic, it should be family policy to keep off the sugar, have lots of high-fibre and low-fat foods and even to use sweeteners in cakes and biscuits. This at least provides a united front with which to face the outside world!

- Try to find alternatives to the unsuitable foods. This is not an easy thing to do, especially having to convince your child that they are unsuitable, but there are compromises. Fruit is an excellent alternative to sweets for snacks and lunches; it is generally sweet tasting, it contains fibre, vitamins and minerals and is certainly the healthier choice. Fruit should be one alternative but variety is important. Home baking is an ideal way of helping your child. What better way of making the diet acceptable than to make delicious sugar-free (preferably low-fat, high-fibre) biscuits that can be shared with friends at school – though always make sure that your child eats the correct carbohydrate allowance and, if necessary, wrap his or her portion separately. Extra fruit in a lunch box that can be shared with friends is also a possibility although this sort of generosity can get rather expensive! If your child does want to buy snacks with friends, recommend the least harmful alternatives. Fruit, again, is the ideal choice but packets of nuts and raisins are a suitable and often preferrable alternative. Packets of crisps and savoury biscuits, although very low in fibre and high in fat, are unlikely to cause hyperglycaemia and are therefore better than sweets. Sugarless chewing gum can also be bought as long as it is understood that chewing gum is an extra and cannot be used to replace a snack. The carbohydrate content of all these foods is given in the BDA's *Countdown* book.
- At all times you should aim to adjust your child to the taste of unsweetened foods and this may be easier than you think – after just one or two weeks, many children are quite used to not having sugar.
- Of course, there are circumstances when diabetics can have sugar. Exercise should be a part of every child's daily routine and should be actively encouraged (though *not* used as a bribe to eat sweets!). The more exercise children get, the more fit and healthy they will be and the more they will be able to eat, including the occasional confectionery bar, before very strenuous exercise.
- One last, very practical point to remember – there will be times when children cheat, for whatever reason. If it is simply that they fancy a packet of sweets and nothing more complex, there is no need to worry. In these circumstances, a little down-to-earth advice on eating a little at a time and eating slowly and at the end of a main meal will probably do as much good as anything. If it starts to become a habit, a

harder line should be taken. Each child in each circumstance is different, and you and your medical advisers will find the best way to cope.

If you and your child follow these suggestions, plus think of ideas for yourselves, you should be able to cope with and enjoy the diabetic diet. Do remember that your doctor or dietitian is there to help with any problem.

THE RECIPES

Analyses
Each recipe has been analysed for its energy, carbohydrate, fibre, protein and fat content. The analysis for fructose is included in the calorie value, not the carbohydrate value. The carbohydrate values have been rounded to the nearest 5 grams. The figures are given per serving where possible. The energy content is given in kilocalories (kcal) and their metric equivalent, kilojoules (kJ). (neg = negligible)

Measurements
Ingredients are given in both metric and imperial measurements, but only use one system yourself; do not combine the two. When spoonfuls are referred to, level spoons are meant.

1 tsp (teaspoon) = 5 ml
1 tbsp (tablespoon) = 15 ml

To ensure success, check the size of the spoons you are using. Australian users should remember that, as their tablespoon has been converted to 20 ml and is therefore larger than the tablespoon measurements used in the recipes in this book, they should use 3 × 5 ml tsp where instructed to use 1 × 15 ml tbsp.

Recipe coding
Each recipe has been clearly coded into one of four categories which relates to the nutritional content of the recipe and therefore how frequently or infrequently it should be included in your controlled diet. All recipes have been made as low in fat and as high in fibre as possible.

★ ★ ★ = This signifies that the recipe is high in carbohydrate and fibre and that its percentage fat content is low. It can therefore be eaten regularly within the confines of your calorie allowance.

★ ★ = This signifies that the recipe has a higher percentage fat content and a correspondingly lower carbohydrate and fibre content. It can be eaten in moderate amounts.

[★] = This signifies that the recipe should be treated with great respect and only eaten on very special occasions, such as birthdays or feast days, because it is higher in fat and therefore has a high calorie content.

[+] =This signifies that the recipe is very low in calories and therefore can be eaten regularly even if you are on a weight-reducing diet.

Try to keep to your personal carbohydrate plan at all times. If you are on a weight-reducing diet, remember that the very low calorie recipes are clearly marked. There are a number of other recipes that have a reasonably low calorie content and can be eaten as long as they are calculated in your daily allowance. Choose those recipes coded with three stars in preference. With their higher fibre content, you will find them more satisfying as well as being better for you.

Suitable for all the family

The wide variety of recipes in this book includes those suitable for everyday cooking and those for special occasions. The appearance and taste of a dish has been an important factor in the development of these recipes. Since the diabetic diet contains little or no sugar (sucrose) and is low-fat and high-fibre, it is very healthy and can be adopted by all members of the family, especially those on a weight-reducing diet.

Sweeteners (see page 18)

The type of sweetening agent used does vary from one recipe to another, but use intense sweeteners in preference to bulk sweeteners wherever possible.

Sugar (sucrose) in non-diabetic cooking provides sweetness and texture, and is used as a preservative and a bulking agent. Alternative sweeteners can provide both sweetness and bulk to recipes, but they do not act as such effective preservatives, and do not provide the expected texture of recipes using sugar – for example, biscuits made with artificial sweeteners are often soft, not crisp.

- Artificially sweetened food may not keep as well so try to eat cakes, biscuits and desserts within 1 or 2 days of cooking. Cakes will not keep well even in an airtight container so any cakes not eaten can be frozen in a freezer or the freezer compartment of a fridge until required. Biscuits and bread can be freshened and crisped in a warm oven before eating.

- Other recipes, such as Spiced mincemeat and Christmas pudding (see pages 116 and 114), should be frozen until required and then kept in the refrigerator for no more than 1–2 days before use.

Frozen desserts

These present the biggest problem in diabetic cooking. Traditional ice cream recipes require eggs, sugar and double cream to achieve good results, while sorbets require a large amount of sugar and some egg whites. Sugar and high-fat ingredients, such as cream, are not suitable for a diabetic diet, so ice cream recipes have been omitted and sorbet recipes have been adapted to achieve similar results.

General tips on ingredients and food preparation for a healthy diet

- **To ensure you eat a high-fibre diet:** use wholemeal flour in preference to white flour (or half wholemeal/half white); try to introduce the interesting nutty flavours of wholegrain products as well as wholemeal flour – for example, add oats and breadcrumbs to a crumble topping; eat plenty of fruit, nuts, cereals and grains; leave skins on fresh fruit where possible; a wide variety of frozen and canned fruit is available and can be substituted for fresh fruit, but check that canned fruit is canned in natural juice and not sugar syrup; use an electric blender for processing food rather than a sieve to ensure you do not lose valuable fibre – also, do not blend to too fine a purée to keep fibre intact.
- **To ensure you eat a low-fat diet:** use polyunsaturated margarines, low-fat spreads, polyunsaturated oils, such as corn, soya and sunflower, but use them all sparingly; since fat in pastry and baking recipes provides moisture and some crispness, try to eat the recipes on the day of cooking to retain freshness – they are often better warmed in the oven; use skimmed milk or reconstituted dried skimmed milk instead of whole milk; use low-fat skimmed milk cheeses, such as cottage cheese, low-fat curd cheese and Fromage blanc – these are often good for fillings, toppings and alternatives to cream; use low-fat plain yoghurts or low-fat fruit yoghurts without added sugar. Instead of glazing pastry, be creative with the pastry trimmings and decorate the top of the pie or flan with pastry leaves and roses instead.
- Use Pear and apple spread as an alternative sweetener. This is a commerical product available from most health food stores and is particularly good in cakes.

SPONGE AND FRUIT CAKES

SPONGE CAKES

Whisked sponge cake

Serves 8
Each serving: 105 kcal/442 kJ, 15 g carbohydrate, 1 g fibre, 4 g protein, 2 g fat

polyunsaturated margarine, for greasing
3 eggs, separated
40 g/1½ oz fructose
30 ml/2 tbsp water
75 g/3 oz wholemeal flour
¼ tsp cream of tartar
90 ml/6 tbsp sugar-free strawberry jam
1 tsp icing sugar or powdered sweetener, to sprinkle

Heat the oven to 190°C/375°F/gas 5 and grease and base-line with greaseproof paper two 20 cm/8 inch sandwich tins. Using an electric mixer or hand whisk, whisk the egg yolks, fructose and water in a large bowl until pale and foamy. Fold in the flour.

Whisk the egg whites and cream of tartar in another large bowl until peaks form. Fold the egg whites into the flour mixture. Divide the mixture between the prepared sandwich tins.

Bake for 10–15 minutes until risen and firm to the touch. Cool on a wire tray. Peel off the paper and sandwich the cakes together with the jam. Dredge the top with the icing sugar or powdered sweetener, and serve.

Lemon sandwich cake

Serves 8
Each serving: 211 kcal/886 kJ, 20 g carbohydrate, 1 g fibre, 4 g protein, 12 g fat

115 g/4 oz polyunsaturated margarine, plus extra for greasing
50 g/2 oz fructose
2 eggs
75 g/3 oz self-raising wholemeal flour
grated rind and juice of 1 lemon
75 g/3 oz self-raising flour
½ tsp baking powder
a little skimmed milk
45 ml/3 tbsp sugar-free jam

→

Heat the oven to 170°C/325°F/gas 3 and lightly grease and base-line with greaseproof paper two 18 cm/7 inch sandwich tins.

Cream the margarine and fructose together in a bowl until pale and fluffy. Beat in the eggs, one at a time, adding a little wholemeal flour, if necessary, to prevent the mixture curdling. Stir in the lemon rind.

Sift the white flour and baking powder together and fold into the mixture with the remaining wholemeal flour. Stir in the lemon juice and sufficient skimmed milk to give a dropping consistency.

Divide the mixture between the prepared tins. Level the surface and bake for about 20 minutes until risen and firm to the touch. Leave to cool slightly in the tins, then remove from the tins and cool on a wire tray. Peel off the greaseproof paper and sandwich the cakes together with the jam.

Carrot and nut sponge cake ★

Makes 12 slices **see photograph, page 33**

Each slice: 108 kcal/453 kJ, 5 g carbohydrate, 2 g fibre, 3 g protein, 7 g fat

polyunsaturated margarine, for greasing
115 g/4 oz shelled hazelnuts or almonds, or a mixture of both
25 g/1 oz desiccated coconut
3 eggs, separated
75 g/3 oz fructose
150 g/5 oz carrots, grated
25 g/1 oz wholemeal flour
½ tsp baking powder
grated rind of ½ lemon or orange

Heat the oven to 180°C/350°F/gas 4 and grease and base-line with greaseproof paper an 18 cm/7 inch round cake tin. Place the nuts on a baking sheet and toast in the oven for 10–15 minutes until golden. Add the coconut after 5 minutes and toast for a further 5 minutes until golden. Cool slightly. Grind the mixed nuts in a food processor or rotary grater.

Whisk the egg yolks with two-thirds of the fructose in a bowl until pale and thick. Stir in the ground nuts, grated carrots, flour, baking powder and lemon or orange rind.

In another bowl, whisk the egg whites until stiff, then continue whisking while adding the remaining fructose, a little at a time. Fold the egg white mixture into the cake mixture until evenly mixed. Spoon the mixture into the prepared cake tin. Bake for 40–45 minutes until risen and firm to the touch. Cool in the tin, then transfer to a wire tray to go cold.

Poppy seed cake ★

Serves 16

Each slice: 205 kcal/860 kJ, 10 g carbohydrate, 2 g fibre, 5 g protein, 14 g fat

115 g/4 oz poppy seeds
225 ml/8 fl oz skimmed milk
3 eggs, separated
115 g/4 oz fructose
150 ml/¼ pt sunflower oil, plus extra for greasing
225 g/8 oz wholemeal flour
2 tsp baking powder
pinch of salt

Heat the oven to 170°C/325°F/gas 3 and grease and line with greaseproof paper a 20 cm/8 inch cake tin. Put the poppy seeds and milk in a saucepan and bring to the boil. Remove from heat and leave to stand for 15 minutes.

In a mixing bowl, beat the egg yolks and fructose, then mix in the sunflower oil. Gradually add the dry ingredients, mixing well. Beat in the poppy seeds and milk.

In another bowl, whisk the egg whites with a pinch of salt until stiff, then carefully fold into the mixture.

Pour into the prepared cake tin and bake for about 1¼ hours, until risen and firm. Test by inserting a thin skewer into the centre of the cake. If it comes out clean, the cake is ready. Leave in the tin for 10 minutes then turn out on to a wire tray and leave to go cold.

Serve in slices.

Moist gingerbread

Serves 16
see photograph, page 33

Each serving: 172 kcal/722 kJ, 25 g carbohydrate, 3 g fibre, 4 g protein, 6 g fat

225 g/8 oz Pear and apple spread (see page 28)
300 ml/½ pt skimmed milk
10 ml/2 tsp lemon juice
115 g/4 oz white polyunsaturated vegetable fat, plus extra for greasing
4 tsp ground ginger
1 tsp ground cinnamon
350 g/12 oz wholemeal flour
50 g/2 oz sultanas
2 tsp bicarbonate of soda
30 ml/2 tbsp boiling water
25 g/1 oz flaked almonds

Heat the oven to 180°C/350°F/gas 4 and grease and line with greaseproof paper a 20 cm/8 inch square cake tin. Place the Pear and apple spread, skimmed milk, lemon juice, fat and spices in a saucepan and heat gently until melted.

Mix together the flour and sultanas in a large bowl. Mix together the bicarbonate of soda and boiling water and add to the flour with the skimmed milk mixture. Beat well until evenly mixed, then pour into the prepared cake tin. Sprinkle with the almonds and bake for about 45 minutes until risen and firm to the touch. Cool in the tin, then transfer to a wire tray until cold. Cut in squares to serve.

Plum and almond squares ★

Makes 9

Each square: 125 kcal/525 kJ, 10 g carbohydrate, 1 g fibre, 2 g protein, 7 g fat

50 g/2 oz polyunsaturated margarine, plus extra for greasing
50 g/2 oz fructose
1 egg
25 g/1 oz self-raising wholemeal flour
50 g/2 oz self-raising flour
25 g/1 oz ground almonds
few drops almond or vanilla essence
30–45 ml/2–3 tbsp skimmed milk
4–5 dessert plums, stoned, and cut in quarters
15 ml/1 tbsp flaked almonds

Heat the oven to 170°C/325°F/gas 3 and lightly grease and base-line with greaseproof paper a 19 cm/7½ inch shallow square cake tin. Put the margarine and fructose in a bowl and cream until pale and fluffy. Beat in the egg then fold in the dry ingredients. Stir in the almond or vanilla essence and sufficient milk to mix to a dropping consistency.

Spread the mixture over the base of the prepared tin. Top with the quartered plums and sprinkle with the flaked almonds. Bake for about 25 minutes until risen and firm to the touch. Cool in the tin, then cut into squares.

FRUIT CAKES

Fruit cake loaf ★ ★

Serves 12

Each serving: 288 kcal/1212 kJ, 40 g carbohydrate, 7 g fibre, 5 g protein, 14 g fat

90 ml/6 tbsp skimmed milk
550 g/1¼ lb mixed dried fruits (eg. currants, sultanas, raisins, dates, prunes, apricots, pears, apples), roughly chopped
225 g/8 oz wholemeal flour
2 tsp baking powder
pinch of salt
2 eggs
150 ml/¼ pt sunflower oil, plus extra for greasing

Pour the milk into a bowl. Add the fruit and leave to soak for at least 30 minutes. Heat the oven to 170°C/325°F/gas 3 and grease and line with greaseproof paper a 900 g/2 lb loaf tin.

Mix together the dry ingredients. Beat the eggs and oil together in a bowl. Stir in the dry ingredients and fruit with any milk that has not been absorbed.

Pour the mixture into the prepared loaf tin. Level the surface

---

Moist gingerbread (*top*, see page 31); Carrot and nut sponge (*centre left and bottom*, see page 30); Plum and almond squares (*centre right*)

and bake for 1 hour. Reduce the heat to 150°C/300°F/gas 2 for about 30 minutes. Cover the cake with foil to prevent over browning, if necessary. Test by inserting a thin skewer into the centre of the cake. If it comes out clean, the cake is cooked. Cool the cake in the tin, then transfer to a wire tray. Leave to go cold. Serve in slices.

Boiled fruit cake ★ ★

Makes 16 slices

Each slice: 171 kcal/719 kJ, 25 g carbohydrate, 3 g fibre, 3 g protein, 5 g fat

300 ml/½ pt freshly made tea
175 g/6 oz currants
175 g/6 oz sultanas
15 ml/1 tbsp ground mixed spice
115 g/4 oz polyunsaturated margarine, plus extra for greasing
50 g/2 oz fructose
275 g/10 oz plain flour (preferably half wholemeal, half white)
2 tsp bicarbonate of soda
1 large egg, beaten

Place the tea, currants, sultanas, and spice in a saucepan and bring to the boil. Reduce the heat and simmer for 20 minutes. Stir in the margarine and leave to cool. Heat the oven to 170°C/325°F/gas 3 and grease and base-line with greaseproof paper a 20 cm/8 inch round cake tin.

Mix together the fructose, flour and bicarbonate of soda in a bowl. Add the fruit mixture and the egg and beat well until evenly mixed.

Spoon the mixture into the cake tin, level the surface and bake for about 1 hour until risen and firm to the touch. Cool in the tin then transfer to a wire tray and leave until completely cold.

Boil-in-pan fruit cake ★ ★

Serves 10

Each serving: 148 kcal/621 kJ, 25 g carbohydrate, 3 g fibre, 4 g protein, 5 g fat

50 g/2 oz sultanas
50 g/2 oz raisins
50 g/2 oz currants
50 g/2 oz stoned dates, chopped
50 g/2 oz polyunsaturated margarine, plus extra for greasing
150 ml/¼ pt skimmed milk
1 egg, beaten
150 g/5 oz wholemeal flour
2 tsp baking powder
1 tsp ground cinnamon
1 tsp ground nutmeg
about 60 ml/4 tbsp skimmed milk

→

Cornish saffron bread (*top*, see page 39); Chunky apple cake (*left*, see page 36); Cranberry and pecan teabread (*right*, see page 42)

Heat the oven to 180°C/350°F/gas 4 and grease and line with greaseproof paper an 18 cm/7 inch cake tin. Put the dried fruit, margarine and milk in a saucepan and bring to the boil. Reduce the heat and simmer gently, covered, for 10 minutes. Remove from the heat and allow to cool. Stir in the egg. Gradually mix in the flour, baking powder and spices and sufficient skimmed milk to give a dropping consistency.

Pour the mixture into the prepared cake tin and bake for about 30 minutes, until risen and firm to the touch. Cool on a wire tray.

Australian cake ★ ★

Serves 16

Each serving: 232 kcal/974 kJ, 30 g carbohydrate, 8 g fibre, 6 g protein, 11 g fat

polyunsaturated margarine, for greasing
175 g/6 oz stoned dates
50 g/2 oz ready-to-eat stoned prunes
115 g/4 oz dried pears, quartered
175 g/6 oz dried peaches or apricots, quartered
grated rind and juice of 1 large orange
50 g/2 oz raisins
75 g/3 oz unblanched almonds
175 g/6 oz shelled walnuts
75 g/3 oz shelled hazelnuts
175 g/6 oz wholemeal flour
pinch of salt
1 tsp baking powder
3 eggs, beaten
1 tsp vanilla essence
30 ml/2 tbsp sugar-free apricot jam, sieved and warmed

Heat the oven to 150°C/300°F/gas 2 and grease and line with greaseproof paper a 900 g/2 lb loaf tin.

Mix all the fruit and nuts together. Mix the flour, salt and baking powder in a bowl. Add the fruit and nut mixture to the flour and toss well to coat evenly.

Add the eggs and vanilla essence and mix well. Spoon the mixture into the prepared tin and press down with the back of a spoon.

Bake for about 1 hour, until firm and golden. Test by inserting a skewer into the centre of the cake. If it comes out clean the cake is cooked. Cool in the tin. Turn out the cake and glaze the top with the apricot jam.

Chunky apple cake ★

Makes 12 slices see photograph, page 34

Each slice: 185 kcal/776 kJ, 15 g carbohydrate, 3 g fibre, 3 g protein, 10 g fat

200 g/7 oz wholemeal flour
pinch of salt
½ tsp ground cinnamon
½ tsp bicarbonate of soda
100 ml/4 fl oz sunflower oil, plus extra for greasing
75 g/3 oz fructose
1 large egg
450 g/1 lb cooking apples, peeled, cored and thinly sliced
50 g/2 oz raisins
25 g/1 oz shelled walnuts, chopped
15 ml/1 tbsp skimmed milk or water

Heat the oven to 180°C/350°F/gas 4 and lightly grease a 24 cm/9½ inch ring tin (1.5 litre/2½ pt capacity). Mix together the flour, salt, cinnamon, and bicarbonate of soda.

Put the oil and fructose in a bowl and beat together until well mixed. Beat in the egg until the mixture is creamy. Stir in the flour mixture, apples, raisins, walnuts and milk or water. The mixture will be very 'chunky'.

Spoon the mixture into the prepared tin and bake for about 40 minutes or until risen and firm to the touch. Allow to cool in the tin, then turn out and serve either at room temperature or cold, cut in slices.

Orange, raisin and almond cake ★ ★

Makes 12 squares

Each serving: 136 kcal/573 kJ, 15 g carbohydrate, 1 g fibre, 6 g protein, 6 g fat

75 g/3 oz raisins, very finely chopped
15 ml/1 tbsp grated orange rind
50 g/2 oz polyunsaturated margarine, plus extra for greasing
40 g/1½ oz skimmed milk powder
1 egg
150 g/5 oz plain flour
1½ tsp baking powder
100 ml/4 fl oz orange juice
50 g/2 oz flaked or nibbed almonds, toasted

Sauce:
60 ml/4 tbsp fructose
60 ml/4 tbsp orange juice
12 fresh orange segments, to decorate (optional)

Heat the oven to 170°C/325°F/gas 3 and grease and base-line a 20 cm/8 inch square cake tin. Mix together the raisins and orange rind. Cream the margarine and skimmed milk powder in a bowl. Beat in the egg, and then the raisin mixture.

Sift the flour and baking powder together and fold in alternating with the orange juice. Fold in the almonds.

Spoon the mixture into the prepared cake tin, level the surface and bake for about 30 minutes until risen and firm to the touch.

To make the sauce, put the fructose and orange juice in a small saucepan and bring to a rapid boil. Prick the top of the cake with a fine skewer and pour the orange sauce over. Leave to go cold in the tin, then cut into squares to serve. Decorate with fresh orange segments if wished.

Orange and caraway towers ★

Makes 10

Each tower: 160 kcal/673 kJ, 15 g carbohydrate, 1 g fibre, 3 g protein, 9 g fat

75 g/3 oz polyunsaturated margarine, plus extra for greasing
50 g/2 oz fructose
105 ml/7 tbsp sugar-free marmalade
grated rind of 1 orange
2 eggs, beaten
115 g/4 oz self-raising flour (preferably half white, half wholemeal)
1–2 tsp caraway seeds
about 45 ml/3 tbsp desiccated coconut

Heat the oven to 170°C/325°F/gas 3 and lightly grease ten dariole moulds. Put the margarine and fructose in a bowl and cream until pale and fluffy. Beat in 30 ml/2 tbsp of the marmalade, and the grated orange rind. Gradually beat in the eggs. Fold in the flour and caraway seeds.

Divide the mixture between the prepared moulds. Bake for about 20–25 minutes, until risen and firm to the touch. Remove from the moulds and leave to cool on a wire tray. Warm and sieve the remaining marmalade. Brush each cake with the marmalade and roll in the desiccated coconut to cover evenly.

BREADS, TEABREADS AND PASTRIES

BREADS

Cornish saffron bread ★ ★ ★

Makes 16 slices **see photograph, page 34**

Each slice: 138 kcal/579 kJ, 25 g carbohydrate, 2 g fibre, 3 g protein, 3 g fat

3 generous pinches of saffron strands
150 ml/¼ pt boiling water
25 g/1 oz fresh yeast or 15 g/½ oz dried yeast
150 ml/¼ pt lukewarm skimmed milk
15 ml/1 tbsp fructose
450 g/1 lb strong plain flour
1 tsp salt
50 g/2 oz polyunsaturated margarine, plus extra for greasing
115 g/4 oz currants
finely grated rind of 1 lemon

Grease a 20 cm/8 inch round cake tin. Soak the saffron in the boiling water. Put the yeast in a small bowl with the milk and, if using dried yeast, stir in the fructose at this stage. Leave in a warm place for about 15 minutes until frothy.

Put the flour, salt (and fructose if using fresh yeast) in a large bowl. Rub in the margarine then add the currants and lemon rind. Mix to a soft dough with the saffron liquid and the yeast. Knead quickly on a lightly floured surface. Press the dough into the prepared cake tin, cover with oiled polythene and leave in a warm place for about 1 hour until the mixture has risen almost to the top of the tin. Heat the oven to 200°C/400°F/gas 6.

Bake for 30 minutes. Reduce the heat to 180°C/350°F/gas 4 and bake for a further 30 minutes. Turn out and cool on a wire tray. When cold, serve in slices spread lightly with polyunsaturated margarine or low-fat spread.

Cottage cheese bread ★ ★ ★

Makes 14 slices

Each slice: 94 kcal/394 kJ, 15 g carbohydrate, 1 g fibre, 4 g protein, 2 g fat

→

175 g/6 oz cottage cheese, sieved
1 egg
grated rind of 1 orange
225 g/8 oz plain flour
2 tsp baking powder
pinch of salt
30 ml/2 tbsp finely chopped dried figs
15 ml/1 tbsp raisins
15 ml/1 tbsp nibbed almonds
15 g/½ oz polyunsaturated margarine, melted, plus extra for greasing

Heat the oven to 180°C/350°F/gas 4 and lightly grease a baking sheet. Put the cottage cheese, egg and orange rind in a bowl and beat well. Sift the dry ingredients into another bowl. Stir in the figs, raisins and almonds. Add the cheese mixture and mix to a firm dough.

Knead on a lightly floured surface. Shape to an oval about 20 cm/8 inch long and 2.5 cm/1 inch deep. Place the dough on the baking sheet and bake for 30 minutes. Reduce the heat to 170°C/325°F/gas 3 and cook for a further 20 minutes. Cover with foil if the bread becomes too brown.

Transfer the bread to a wire tray and brush the surface with margarine. Leave until completely cold. Serve cut in thin slices and spread thinly with polyunsaturated margarine or low-fat spread.

Soda bread ★ ★ ★

Serves 8

Each serving: 195 kcal/817 kJ, 40 g carbohydrate, 5 g fibre, 9 g protein, 1 g fat

polyunsaturated margarine, for greasing
450 g/1 lb wholemeal flour
½ tsp salt
½ tsp bicarbonate of soda
½ tsp cream of tartar
300 ml/½ pt buttermilk

Heat the oven to 220°C/425°F/gas 7 and lightly grease a baking sheet. Mix together all the dry ingredients in a bowl. Stir in the buttermilk and mix to a firm dough. Knead on a lightly floured surface. Shape into a round about 20 cm/8 inch in diameter. Place the dough on the baking sheet and cut a deep cross through the centre.

Bake for about 30 minutes, until risen and firm. To check if the bread is cooked through, tap the underside with your knuckles; it should sound hollow. Allow to cool on a wire tray. Serve fresh on the day of making.

Surprise hazelnut plait ★ ★

Makes 16 slices

Each slice: 87 kcal/364 kJ, 10g carbohydrate, 1 g fibre, 2 g protein, 4 g fat

175 g/6 oz plain flour
25 g/1 oz wheatgerm
pinch of salt
40 g/1½ oz polyunsaturated margarine, plus extra for greasing
15 g/½ oz fresh yeast, or 7 g/¼ oz dried yeast
15 g/½ oz fructose
50 ml/2 fl oz lukewarm skimmed milk
1 egg, beaten

Filling:
50 g/2 oz shelled hazelnuts, toasted and chopped
25 g/1 oz raisins, roughly chopped
30 ml/2 tbsp sugar-free cherry jam (or any other flavour)

Lightly grease a baking sheet. Sift the flour into a bowl. Stir in the wheatgerm and salt. Rub in 25 g/1 oz of the margarine. Mix the yeast with the fructose and milk in a cup and leave in a warm place for 15 minutes or until frothy.

Add the yeast mixture and egg to the flour and mix to a soft dough. Knead on a lightly floured surface for 5 minutes. Return the dough to the lightly oiled bowl, cover and leave in a warm place to rise for about 30–45 minutes or until doubled in size. Turn out the dough, knead for a minute or two then roll out to a rectangle 30 × 23 cm/12 × 9 inch and mark into three sections crossways.

Mix the ingredients for the filling and spread this over the central section of dough. Cut the two outside sections into 1.5 cm/¾ inch wide slanting strips. Fold in the top and bottom pieces of dough then fold in the strips alternately to give a plaited effect. Place the plait on the baking sheet. Cover and leave in a warm place for 15 minutes. Heat the oven to 220°C/425°F/gas 7. Bake for 10 minutes, reduce the heat to 190°C/375°F/gas 5 and bake for a further 10–15 minutes.

Brush with the remaining margarine to glaze. Cool on a wire tray. Serve fresh, cut in slices.

TEABREADS

Banana walnut teabread ★ ★

Makes 12 slices
Each slice: 180 kcal/756 kJ, 20 g carbohydrate, 2 g fibre, 3 g protein, 8 g fat

75 g/3 oz polyunsaturated margarine, plus extra for greasing
75 g/3 oz fructose
1 egg, beaten
2 large ripe bananas, mashed
225 g/8 oz plain flour (preferably half white, half wholemeal)
pinch of salt
15 ml/1 tbsp baking powder
50 g/2 oz shelled walnuts, chopped

→

Heat the oven to 170°C/325°F/gas 3 and grease and base-line with greaseproof paper a 900 g/2 lb loaf tin. Put the margarine and fructose in a bowl and beat until pale and fluffy. Beat in the egg and bananas. Mix the flour, salt and baking powder together and fold in with the nuts. Spoon the mixture into the prepared loaf tin. Level the surface.

Bake for about 50 minutes until risen and firm to the touch. Cool in the tin, then transfer to a wire tray. Leave until completely cold. Serve in slices.

Apricot and almond teabread

Makes 12 slices

Each slice: 182 kcal/763 kJ, 20 g carbohydrate, 3 g fibre, 4 g protein, 8 g fat

75 g/3 oz polyunsaturated margarine, plus extra for greasing
75 g/3 oz fructose
1 egg
½ tsp almond essence
115 g/4 oz dried apricots, finely chopped
50 g/2 oz nibbed almonds
225 g/8 oz self-raising flour
100 ml/4 fl oz skimmed milk

Heat the oven to 170°C/325°F/gas 3 and grease and base-line with greaseproof paper a 900 g/2 lb loaf tin. Put the margarine and fructose in a bowl and cream until pale and fluffy. Beat in the egg and almond essence. Fold in the apricots, almonds and flour, and mix to a soft dough with the milk.

Transfer the mixture to the prepared tin. Level the surface and bake for about 50 minutes until risen and firm. Cool in the tin, then transfer to a wire tray and leave until completely cold. Serve in slices, spread thinly with polyunsaturated margarine or low-fat spread.

Cranberry and pecan teabread

Makes 16 slices **see photograph, page 34**

Each slice: 126 kcal/529 kJ, 10 g carbohydrate, 1 g fibre, 3 g protein, 5 g fat

225 g/8 oz plain flour (preferably half wholemeal, half white)
2 tsp baking powder
50 g/2 oz polyunsaturated margarine, plus extra for greasing
115 g/4 oz fructose
115 g/4 oz cranberries
75 g/3 oz pecan nuts, chopped
1 egg, beaten
100 ml/4 fl oz skimmed milk

Heat the oven to 170°C/325°F/gas 3 and grease and base-line with greaseproof paper a 900 g/2 lb loaf tin. Mix together the flour and baking powder in a bowl and rub in the margarine. Stir in the fructose, cranberries, two-thirds of the pecans and mix to a soft dough with the egg and milk. Transfer the mixture to the loaf tin and level the surface.

Sprinkle with the remaining pecans and bake for about 1 hour until risen and firm to the touch. Cool in the tin, then place on a wire tray. Serve in slices, spread thinly with polyunsaturated margarine or low-fat spread.

Spicy fruit teabread ★ ★ ★

Makes 12 slices

Each slice: 162 kcal/680 kJ, 35 g carbohydrate, 3 g fibre, 4 g protein, 1 g fat

polyunsaturated margarine, for greasing
115 g/4 oz each currants, sultanas and raisins
freshly made tea, to soak
175 g/6 oz wholemeal flour
175 g/6 oz self-raising flour
2 tsp baking powder
25 g/1 oz fructose
2 tsp ground mixed spice
¼ tsp aniseed
grated rind of ½ lemon
1 egg, beaten

Grease and base-line with greaseproof paper a 900 g/2 lb loaf tin. Put the dried fruit in a bowl and cover generously with freshly made tea. Cover and leave to soak for at least 12 hours. Heat the oven to 190°C/375°F/gas 5.

Drain the fruit, reserving 150 ml/¼ pt of the soaking liquid for this recipe*. Place all the ingredients in a bowl and beat well for 2 minutes until evenly mixed. Transfer the mixture into the prepared loaf tin. Level the surface and bake for about 1¼ hours, until risen and firm to the touch. To test if the loaf is cooked, insert a metal skewer into the centre; if it comes out clean the teabread is ready.

Allow to cool, then transfer to a wire tray. Leave until completely cold, then serve in slices, with a thin spreading of polyunsaturated margarine or low-fat spread.

* Do keep the rest of the liquid – chilled, it makes a delicious drink, either on its own, or with added soda.

PASTRIES

Basic wholemeal pastry ★

Makes 350 g/12 oz

Total recipe: 1382 kcal/5804 kJ, 135 g carbohydrate, 19 g fibre, 27 g protein, 85 g fat

→

200 g/7 oz wholemeal flour
2 tsp baking powder
100 g/3½ oz polyunsaturated margarine
45 ml/3 tbsp cold water

Put the flour and baking powder in a bowl and rub in the margarine until the mixture resembles fine crumbs. Stir in the water and mix to a firm dough.

Chill and use as required.

Quick bread pastry dough ★ ★ ★

Makes 350–400 g/12–14 oz
Total recipe: 769 kcal/3230 kJ, 150 g carbohydrate, 23 g fibre, 31 g protein, 10 g fat

225 g/8 oz plain flour (all wholemeal or half wholemeal and half white)
pinch of salt
5 ml/1 tsp polyunsaturated oil
1 tsp easy blend dried yeast
about 150 ml/¼ pt lukewarm water

Place the flour, salt, oil and dried yeast in a bowl. Mix in sufficient water to make a manageable dough. Knead on a lightly floured surface, then wrap in a polythene bag and refrigerate until required.

Raspberry profiteroles ★

Makes 20 **see photograph, page 51**
Each profiterole: 73 kcal/307 kJ, 10 g carbohydrate, 1 g fibre, 2 g protein, 4 g fat

150 ml/¼ pt water
50 g/2 oz polyunsaturated margarine
65 g/2½ oz wholemeal flour
pinch of salt
2 medium eggs, beaten

Filling:
1 quantity Pastry cream (see page 110)

Sauce:
150 ml/¼ pt orange or any other fruit juice
150 ml/¼ pt water
2 tsp arrowroot
50 g/2 oz chocolate, broken into pieces
20 fresh raspberries or cherries, to decorate

Heat the oven to 200°C/400°F/gas 6 and grease a baking tray.

In a saucepan, heat the water and margarine, until the margarine melts and the water boils. Remove from the heat and beat in the flour and salt. Cool slightly and beat in the eggs. Continue beating until the mixture is smooth and glossy. Spoon or pipe twenty walnut-sized pieces of pastry on to the baking tray. Bake for 10 minutes, then reduce the temperature to 180°C/350°F/gas 4 and bake for a further 25 minutes. Make a slit in each bun to release the steam and ensure the pastry remains crisp.

To make the sauce, mix the orange juice and water together in a saucepan. Whisk in the arrowroot and cook, stirring, until thickened. Remove from the heat and whisk in the chocolate to make a smooth sauce.

To serve, pipe or spoon the cold Pastry cream into each choux bun. Decorate each with a fresh raspberry or cherry. Pour some sauce over the buns and serve the remainder separately.

Amanda's apple strudel ★ ★

Serves 8

Each serving: 160 kcal/674 kJ, 20 g carbohydrate, 3 g fibre, 4 g protein, 7 g fat

115 g/4 oz wholemeal flour
15 ml/1 tbsp polyunsaturated oil
1 small egg, beaten
30–45 ml/2–3 tbsp water

Filling:
25 g/1 oz polyunsaturated margarine
25 g/1 oz toasted breadcrumbs
25 g/1 oz ground almonds
50 g/2 oz raisins
2 tsp ground cinnamon
450 g/1 lb cooking or dessert apples, peeled, cored and thinly sliced

Heat the oven to 200°C/400°F/gas 6.

Place the flour in a bowl, add the oil, egg and sufficient water to mix to a fairly soft, yet manageable dough. Roll out the dough on a lightly floured clean tea towel as thinly as possible to a large rectangle. Spread with a generous half of the margarine and then sprinkle with the breadcrumbs, ground almonds, raisins and cinnamon. Place the apple slices along the length of the pastry. Fold in the ends, then fold over first one side, and then the other to encase the apples completely. Press the edges well to seal.

Transfer the apple strudel to a non-stick baking tray, spread with the remaining margarine and bake for about 25 minutes until the apples are tender when tested with a skewer, and the pastry is crisp. Serve warm or cold cut in slices.

MUFFINS, SCONES AND BUNS

MUFFINS

English muffins ★ ★ ★

Makes 12 see photograph, page 51
Each muffin: 155 kcal/651 kJ, 25 g carbohydrate, 4 g fibre, 7 g protein, 3 g fat

450 g/1 lb wholemeal flour
1 tsp salt
1 standard pkt easy blend dried yeast
25 g/1 oz polyunsaturated white fat, plus extra for greasing
150 ml/¼ pt skimmed milk
150 ml/¼ pt water
1 egg, beaten
30 ml/2 tbsp semolina

Lightly grease a baking sheet. Mix together the flour, salt and yeast in a bowl. Rub in the fat. Heat the milk and water together until just tepid. Add to the flour with the egg and mix to a dough. Turn out and knead well for at least 10 minutes. Alternatively, work the dough in a food processor until smooth and elastic.

Transfer to a lightly oiled bowl, cover with oiled polythene and leave in a warm place for 45–50 minutes to rise until doubled in size.

On a lightly floured surface, roll out the dough to about 2 cm/¾ inch thick. Stamp out twelve 7.5 cm/3 inch rounds, using the trimmings and rerolling as necessary. Sprinkle the baking sheet with half the semolina and arrange the muffins on it. Sprinkle the remaining semolina over the muffins and cover with oiled polythene. Leave in a warm place to rise for about 30 minutes. Heat the oven to 200°C/400°F/gas 6 and bake for 15 minutes until firm to the touch and hollow-sounding when tapped. Serve warm.

Bran and raisin muffins ★ ★

Makes 9
Each muffin: 106 kcal/444 kJ, 15 g carbohydrate, 2 g fibre, 3 g protein, 4 g fat

100 g/3½ oz oat germ and oat bran
40 g/1½ oz wholemeal flour
¼ tsp salt
1½ tsp baking powder
1 tsp mixed spice
50 g/2 oz raisins
1 egg, beaten
125 ml/4½ fl oz skimmed milk
25 ml/1½ tbsp sunflower oil, plus extra for greasing

Heat the oven to 200°C/400°F/gas 6 and lightly oil nine muffin tins. Mix all the dry ingredients together in a bowl. Add the raisins and mix well. Mix in the egg, milk and oil and leave to stand for a short while.

Pour the batter into the muffin tins; they should be only two-thirds full. Bake for about 15 minutes, or until golden and firm to the touch. Serve warm.

Blueberry muffins ★ ★

Makes 12

see photograph, page 51

Each muffin: 90 kcal/378 kJ, 10 g carbohydrate, 1 g fibre, 3 g protein, 3 g fat

175 g/6 oz wholemeal flour
1½ tsp baking powder
25 g/1 oz fructose
1 egg, beaten
30 ml/2 tbsp sunflower oil, plus extra for greasing
60–75 ml/4–5 tbsp skimmed milk
115 g/4 oz blueberries, defrosted if frozen

Heat the oven to 200°C/400°F/gas 6 and lightly oil twelve patty tins. Put the flour, baking powder and fructose in a bowl and mix until evenly combined. Add the egg, sunflower oil and skimmed milk to give a soft dropping consistency. Stir in the blueberries.

Divide the mixture between the patty tins and bake for 10–15 minutes until risen and firm to the touch. Remove from the tins and serve warm.

SCONES

St Clement's scones ★ ★

Makes 16

Each scone: 75 kcal/317 kJ, 10 g carbohydrate, 1 g fibre, 2 g protein, 3 g fat

115 g/4 oz self-raising flour
115 g/4 oz wholemeal flour
1½ tsp baking powder
50 g/2 oz polyunsaturated margarine, plus extra for greasing
25 g/1 oz fructose
grated rind of ½ orange
grated rind of ½ lemon
1 egg, beaten
45–60 ml/3–4 tbsp skimmed milk or buttermilk

→

Heat the oven to 220°C/425°F/gas 7 and lightly grease two baking sheets. In a bowl, mix together the flours and baking powder. Rub in the margarine until the mixture resembles fine crumbs. Add the fructose and the orange and lemon rind and mix well. Mix in the beaten egg and milk or buttermilk to make a firm dough.

On a lightly floured surface, roll out the dough to about 1–2 cm/½–¾ inch thickness and stamp out rounds with a 6 cm/2½ inch cutter. Arrange on the baking sheets and bake for about 10 minutes until golden and firm to the touch. Cool on a wire tray.

Note: Best served on the day of making.

Yoghurt scones

Serves 8

Each scone: 104 kcal/438 kJ, 20 g carbohydrate, 2 g fibre, 4 g protein, 1 g fat

polyunsaturated margarine, for greasing
225 g/8 oz plain flour (preferably half wholemeal, half white)
½ tsp baking powder
¼ tsp bicarbonate of soda
pinch of salt
15 ml/1 tbsp fructose
150 g/5 oz low-fat plain yoghurt
45–60 ml/3–4 tbsp cold water

Heat the oven to 190°C/375°F/gas 5 and lightly grease a baking sheet. Mix together the dry ingredients in a bowl. Mix to a smooth dough with the yoghurt and water. Knead on a lightly floured surface. Pat into an 18 cm/7 inch round. Place on the baking sheet, and mark into eight sections with a sharp knife.

Bake for 25–30 minutes until risen and firm. Break into wedges and serve warm.

Sultana scone triangles

Makes 8

Each triangle: 155 kcal/652 kJ, 25 g carbohydrate, 3 g fibre, 4 g protein, 3 g fat

225 g/8 oz self-raising flour (either all wholemeal or half wholemeal, half white)
25 g/1 oz polyunsaturated margarine
25 g/1 oz fructose
75 g/3 oz sultanas
150 ml/¼ pt buttermilk

Heat the oven to 200°C/400°F/gas 6. Put the flour in a bowl and rub in the margarine. Stir in the fructose and sultanas and mix to a firm dough with the buttermilk. Knead quickly, on a lightly floured board. Shape to a 20 cm/8 inch circle. Cut out eight triangles and place on a non-stick baking sheet.

Bake for 10–15 minutes until risen and golden.

Note: Best served on day of making, preferably while still warm.

Lemon drop scones ★ ★

Makes 12

Each scone: 53 kcal/222 kJ, 5 g carbohydrate, 1 g fibre, 2 g protein, 2 g fat

115 g/4 oz wholemeal flour
1 tsp baking powder
¼ tsp salt
15 g/½ oz polyunsaturated margarine, plus extra for greasing
25 g/1 oz fructose
1 egg, beaten
90–105 ml/6–7 tbsp skimmed milk
½ tsp grated lemon rind

In a mixing bowl, mix the flour, baking powder and salt together. Add the margarine, fructose and beaten egg. Mix together well and beat in enough milk to make a thick batter. Finally mix in the lemon rind.

Heat a lightly greased griddle. Drop spoonfuls of the batter on to the griddle and cook, turning once, for about 5 minutes, until golden on both sides.

Note: Drop scones are best eaten while still warm.

Singing hinny ★ ★

Serves 10

Each serving: 169 kcal/710 kJ, 20 g carbohydrate, 2 g fibre, 3 g protein, 8 g fat

225 g/8 oz plain flour (preferably half wholemeal, half white)
pinch of salt
115 g/4 oz polyunsaturated margarine, plus extra for greasing
75 g/3 oz currants
60–75 ml/4–5 tbsp skimmed milk

Put the flour and salt in a bowl. Rub in the margarine until the mixture resembles fine crumbs. Stir in the currants and mix to a firm dough with the milk. Turn out and knead gently. Flatten to a 18–20 cm/7–8 inch round shape, about 1 cm/½ inch thick.

Heat and lightly grease a heavy-based frying pan or griddle. Place the hinny in the pan and prick all over with a fork. Cook over medium heat, turning once, for about 15 minutes. Serve warm, cut in wedges.

BUNS

Spice buns ★ ★ ★

Makes 12

Each bun: 198 kcal/832 kJ, 35 g carbohydrate, 4 g fibre, 6 g protein, 4 g fat

225 g/8 oz wholemeal flour
225 g/8 oz strong plain flour
1 tsp salt
1 pkt easy blend dried yeast
15 ml/1 tbsp ground mixed spice
50 g/2 oz polyunsaturated white vegetable fat, plus extra for greasing
50 g/2 oz currants
50 g/2 oz sultanas
50 g/2 oz stoned dates, chopped
¼ tsp grated orange rind
¼ tsp grated lemon rind
150 ml/¼ pt skimmed milk
150 ml/¼ pt water
1 egg, beaten

Lightly grease a baking sheet. Mix together the flours, salt, yeast, and mixed spice in a bowl. Rub in the fat. Add the currants, sultanas, dates and orange and lemon rind.

Warm the milk and water together and add to the dry ingredients with the beaten egg. Mix to a dough and knead for at least 10 minutes until smooth. Alternatively, omit the fruit and work the dough in a food processor, until smooth and elastic, then work in the fruit.

Place the dough in a lightly oiled bowl. Cover with oiled polythene and leave in a warm place for 45–60 minutes or until doubled in size. Punch down the dough, turn out on to a lightly floured surface and knead well. Shape into twelve buns. Place on the baking sheet and cover with oiled polythene. Leave to rise in a warm place for 20–30 minutes. Heat the oven to 200°C/400°F/gas 6. When well risen, bake the buns for about 15 minutes or until firm, and hollow sounding when tapped on the base. Cool on a wire tray.

Hot cross buns ★ ★

Makes 12

Each bun: 255 kcal/1073 kJ, 40 g carbohydrate, 4 g fibre, 7 g protein, 8 g fat

To make Hot cross buns, follow the recipe for Spice buns (see above) and make half quantity of Basic wholemeal pastry (see page 43). Roll the pastry out on a lightly floured surface and cut twenty-four long thin strips. Shape the buns then press two strips

---

Raspberry profiteroles (*top*, see page 44); Blueberry muffins (*centre*, see page 47); English muffins (*bottom*, see page 46)

of pastry on to each bun to form a cross. Cover and leave to rise, then brush lightly with beaten egg.

Bake as described for Spice buns (see opposite).

BISCUITS

Oatcakes

★ ★

Makes 24

Each oatcake: 50 kcal/210 kJ, 5 g carbohydrate, 1 g fibre, 1 g protein, 2 g fat

200 g/7 oz fine oatmeal
25 g/1 oz plain flour
½ tsp baking powder
¼ tsp salt
50 g/2 oz polyunsaturated margarine, melted
about 60 ml/4 tbsp boiling water

Heat the oven to 180°C/350°F/gas 4.

Mix the dry ingredients together in a bowl. Stir in the margarine and sufficient boiling water to mix to a firm dough.

Sprinkle the work surface with a little fine oatmeal and roll out the dough to about 3 mm/⅛ inch thickness. Stamp out twenty-four 6 cm/2¼ inch rounds, using the trimmings and rerolling as required. Arrange on a non-stick baking tray and bake for about 20 minutes. Cool on a wire tray.

Hazelnut cookies

★

Makes 18

Each cookie: 69 kcal/292 kJ, 5 g carbohydrate, 1 g fibre, 1 g protein, 4 g fat

75 g/3 oz polyunsaturated margarine, plus extra for greasing
50 g/2 oz dried apricots, minced
2 egg yolks
60 ml/4 tbsp unsweetened pineapple juice
25 g/1 oz hazelnuts, coarsely ground
140 g/4½ oz wholemeal flour

Heat the oven to 170°C/325°F/gas 3 and lightly grease two baking sheets. Put the margarine and apricots in a bowl and mix together. Beat in the egg yolks and pineapple juice. Add the nuts and flour and blend thoroughly. →

Cinnamon cherry sandwiches (*top*, see page 55); Hazelnut cookies (*centre left*); Chocolate chip crunchies (*centre right*, see page 55); Oatcakes, served with low-fat Cheddar cheese (*bottom*)

Place tablespoonfuls of the mixture on to the baking sheets and bake for about 25 minutes, until firm and golden. Cool on a wire tray.

Oat and nut cookies

Makes 18

Each cookie: 63 kcal/267 kJ, 5 g carbohydrate, 1 g fibre, 1 g protein, 4 g fat

75 g/3 oz rolled oats
25 g/1 oz desiccated coconut
50 g/2 oz ground almonds
25 g/1 oz polyunsaturated margarine
1 egg
30 ml/2 tbsp Pear and apple spread *(see page 28)*
½ tsp vanilla essence

Heat the oven to 170°C/325°F/gas 3.

Combine all the ingredients together in a bowl until evenly mixed. Shape into eighteen balls, then flatten each one on to a non-stick baking sheet. Bake for about 15 minutes until golden at the edges. Cool on a wire tray.

Peanut butter cookies

Makes 24

Each cookie: 77 kcal/323 kJ, 10 g carbohydrate, 1 g fibre, 2 g protein, 4 g fat

50 g/2 oz polyunsaturated margarine, plus extra for greasing
50 g/2 oz peanut butter
115 g/4 oz raisins, minced
1 egg, beaten
60 ml/4 tbsp water
1 tsp vanilla essence
200 g/7 oz wholemeal flour
½ tsp baking powder
1 tsp bicarbonate of soda
a little skimmed milk
50 g/2 oz salted peanuts, chopped

Heat the oven to 170°C/325°F/gas 3 and lightly grease two baking sheets.

In a mixing bowl, mix together the margarine, peanut butter and raisins. Add the egg, water and vanilla essence, beating well. Then mix in the flour, baking powder and bicarbonate of soda, until well blended. Place spoonfuls on the baking sheets and flatten slightly. Brush with skimmed milk.

Divide the chopped peanuts between the cookies, pressing them well into each one. Bake for about 15 minutes until firm and golden. Cool on a wire tray.

Country crisp biscuits

Makes 18

Each biscuit: 66 kcal/276 kJ, 10 g carbohydrate, 1 g fibre, 2 g protein, 3 g fat

175 g/6 oz granary or wholemeal flour
40 g/1½ oz coarse oatmeal
1 tsp baking powder
pinch of salt
25 g/1 oz fructose
50 g/2 oz polyunsaturated margarine
30 ml/2 tbsp skimmed milk

Heat the oven to 180°C/350°F/gas 4.

Mix together the flour, oatmeal, baking powder, salt and fructose in a bowl. Rub in the margarine and mix to a firm dough with the milk. Turn out on to a lightly floured surface, and roll out as thinly as possible. Stamp out eighteen 7.5 cm/3 inch rounds, using the trimmings and rerolling as required.

Place on non-stick baking sheets and bake for 15–20 minutes until golden. Cool on a wire tray. Serve with cheese.

Cinnamon cherry sandwiches ★ ★

Makes 12 **see photograph, page 52**

Each biscuit: 103 kcal/433 kJ, 10 g carbohydrate, 1 g fibre, 2 g protein, 4 g fat

50 g/2 oz polyunsaturated margarine
50 g/2 oz fructose
1 egg
½ tsp vanilla essence
1 tsp grated lemon rind
1 tsp ground cinnamon
115 g/4 oz plain flour
50 g/2 oz wholemeal flour
pinch of salt
90 ml/6 tbsp sugar-free cherry or raspberry jam

Topping:
1 tsp fructose
½ tsp ground cinnamon

Heat the oven to 190°C/375°F/gas 5. Put the margarine and fructose in a bowl and cream together until light and fluffy. Beat in the egg, vanilla essence and lemon rind. Mix in the remaining ingredients, except the jam, to make a dough.

Roll out the dough on a lightly floured surface and stamp out twenty-four 7.5 cm/3 inch fluted rounds, using the trimmings and rerolling as necessary. Place on two non-stick baking sheets. To make the topping, mix together the fructose and cinnamon and sprinkle over half the rounds.

Bake for about 10 minutes until lightly browned. Cool on a wire tray. Sandwich the biscuits together with a little of the jam, using all the cinnamon-sprinkled biscuits as the top of each sandwich.

Chocolate chip crunchies ★ ★

Makes 12 **see photograph, page 52**

Each biscuit: 136 kcal/570 kJ, 10 g carbohydrate, 1 g fibre, 3 g protein, 7 g fat

75 g/3 oz polyunsaturated margarine, plus extra for greasing
50 g/2 oz fructose
few drops vanilla essence

→

1 egg, beaten
175 g/6 oz wholemeal flour
1 tsp baking powder
50 g/2 oz chocolate chips

Heat the oven to 170°C/325°F/gas 3 and lightly grease a baking tray.

In a mixing bowl, cream the margarine and fructose until light and fluffy. Add a few drops of vanilla essence and the egg. Beat well, then add the flour and baking powder. Continue beating until well mixed. Mix in the chocolate chips.

Put spoonfuls of the mixture on to the baking tray. Flatten out slightly then bake for about 20 minutes, until golden brown and firm to the touch. Cool on a wire tray.

Crispy crunchies ★

Makes 24

Each biscuit: 64 kcal/271 kJ, 5 g carbohydrate, neg fibre, 1 g protein, 4 g fat

115 g/4 oz polyunsaturated margarine
75 g/3 oz fructose
few drops vanilla essence
1 egg yolk
50 g/2 oz wholemeal flour
75 g/3 oz self-raising flour
½ tsp baking powder
25 g/1 oz Special K or other cereal

Heat the oven to 180°C/350°F/gas 4.

Put the margarine, fructose and vanilla essence in a bowl and cream until pale. Beat in the egg yolk, then work in the flours and baking powder. Form the mixture into twenty-four balls. Roll each one in Special K and place on a non-stick baking tray.

Bake for about 15 minutes until firm and golden. Cool on a wire tray.

Bumble bees ★ ★

Makes 16

see photograph, page 62

Each biscuit: 69 kcal/289 kJ, 10 g carbohydrate, 1 g fibre, 1 g protein, 3 g fat

50 g/2 oz polyunsaturated margarine
225 g/8 oz stoned dates, finely chopped
50 g/2 oz Special K, or Rice Krispies
few drops vanilla essence

Melt the margarine in a saucepan and leave to cool. Stir in the remaining ingredients and squeeze into sixteen 'barrels' with your fingers. Leave to go cold.

Walnutties ★

Makes 20

Each biscuit: 84 kcal/353 kJ, 5 g carbohydrate, 1 g fibre, 2 g protein, 5 g fat

50 g/2 oz polyunsaturated margarine, plus extra for greasing
50 g/2 oz fructose
1 egg
1 tsp vanilla essence
150 g/5 oz plain flour
¼ tsp baking powder
50 g/2 oz shelled walnuts, finely chopped
20 walnut halves

Heat the oven to 180°C/350°F/gas 4 and lightly grease two baking sheets. Put the margarine and fructose in a bowl and cream together until pale and fluffy. Beat in the egg and vanilla essence. Sift the flour and baking powder over the creamed mixture and fold in with the chopped walnuts.

Drop the mixture in spoonfuls on to the baking sheets. Press a walnut half on top of each one. Bake for about 20 minutes until golden. Cool on a wire tray.

PIES AND CRUMBLES

Rhubarb and raspberry pie ★

Serves 8

Each serving: 209 kcal/879 kJ, 20 g carbohydrate, 5 g fibre, 4 g protein, 13 g fat

175 g/6 oz wholemeal flour
25 g/1 oz ground almonds
25 g/1 oz fructose (optional)
115 g/4 oz polyunsaturated margarine
1 egg yolk
30 ml/2 tbsp water
30 ml/2 tbsp ground rice
225 g/8 oz rhubarb, trimmed and cut in 2.5 cm/1 inch lengths
225 g/8 oz raspberries
liquid sweetener, to taste

Heat the oven to 200°C/400°F/gas 6.

Put the flour, ground almonds and fructose, if using, into a bowl. Rub in the margarine until the mixture resembles fine crumbs. Add the egg yolk and water and mix to a firm dough. Lightly knead the pastry. Roll out half the pastry on a lightly floured surface and line a 20 cm/8 inch pie dish. Sprinkle the base with 15 ml/1 tbsp ground rice.

Mix together the rhubarb, raspberries, liquid sweetener, to taste, and the remaining ground rice. Fill the pastry case with the fruit. Roll out the remaining pastry and top the pie. Trim and seal the edges well. Crimp the edges to give a decorative effect. Make a slash in the top of the pie.

Bake for 15 minutes. Reduce the heat to 180°C/350°F/gas 4 and bake for a further 25–30 minutes until the fruit is tender and the pastry crisp. Serve warm or cold.

Traditional apple crumble ★ ★

Serves 4

Each serving: 362 kcal/1520 kJ, 45 g carbohydrate, 6 g fibre, 5 g protein, 16 g fat

Topping:
75 g/3 oz polyunsaturated margarine
175 g/6 oz wholemeal flour
40 g/1½ oz fructose
1 tsp ground coriander

450 g/1 lb cooking apples, peeled, cored and sliced thinly

Heat the oven to 200°C/400°F/gas 6.

Make the topping by rubbing the margarine into the flour, until the mixture resembles coarse breadcrumbs. Add the fructose and coriander and mix together. Set aside.

Put the prepared apples into a 900 ml/1½ pt ovenproof dish. Sprinkle the topping over the apples and bake for 25–30 minutes until the fruit is tender when tested with a skewer.

Crunchy topped crumble ★

Serves 4

Each serving: 298 kcal/1252 kJ, 25 g carbohydrate, 10 g fibre, 6 g protein, 21 g fat

Topping:
75 g/3 oz mixed flakes (e.g. wheat, oat or barley)
25 g/1 oz flaked almonds
25 g/1 oz desiccated coconut
25 g/1 oz sunflower seeds
50 g/2 oz polyunsaturated margarine

450 g/1 lb mixed fruit (e.g. apple, blackberries etc.)

Heat the oven to 200°C/400°F/gas 6. Mix together all the ingredients for the topping.

Put the prepared fruit into a 900 ml/1½ pt ovenproof dish. Cover the fruit with the topping mixture and bake for 25–30 minutes, until the fruit is tender when tested with a skewer.

Blackcurrant and apple crunch ★ ★

Serves 4 **see photograph, page 61**

Each serving: 282 kcal/1183 kJ, 35 g carbohydrate, 8 g fibre, 5 g protein, 12 g fat

225 g/8 oz cooking apples, peeled, cored and thinly sliced
225 g/8 oz blackcurrants
liquid sweetener, to taste

Topping:
115 g/4 oz sugar-free crunchy muesli
50 g/2 oz wholemeal flour
50 g/2 oz polyunsaturated margarine
25 g/1 oz fructose

Heat the oven to 180°C/350°F/gas 4. Mix together the apples, blackcurrants and liquid sweetener and place in a 900 ml/1½ pt ovenproof dish.

Mix together the ingredients for the topping and sprinkle over the fruit. Bake for about 30 minutes, or until the fruit is tender. Serve warm with Pouring custard (see page 112).

Variation: Use 450 g/1 lb of any other fruit or mixture of fruits prepared as necessary instead of blackcurrants and apples.

TARTS AND FLANS

TARTS

Baked cheese tart ★

Serves 10

Each serving: 126 kcal/530 kJ, 10 g carbohydrate, 1 g fibre, 5 g protein, 8 g fat

½ quantity Basic wholemeal pastry (see page 43)
200 g/7 oz low-fat skimmed milk cheese, or cottage cheese
25 g/1 oz polyunsaturated margarine
25 g/1 oz fructose (optional)
50 g/2 oz mixed dried fruit
1 egg
generous pinch of ground nutmeg
½ tsp grated lemon rind
ground cinnamon, to sprinkle

Heat the oven to 190°C/375°F/gas 5.

Roll out the pastry and use to line a 19 cm/7½ inch flan tin. Beat together all the remaining ingredients, except the cinnamon, and pour into the flan tin. Sprinkle the cinnamon over the top and bake for about 25 minutes until just firm. Best served fresh, on the day of making.

Rhubarb and banana tart ★ ★

Serves 8

Each serving: (without topping) 120 kcal/506 kJ, 15 g carbohydrate, 3 g fibre, 2 g protein, 6 g fat
(With topping) 128 kcal/537 kJ, 15 g carbohydrate, 3 g fibre, 3 g protein, 6 g fat

½ quantity Basic wholemeal pastry (see page 43)
175 g/6 oz rhubarb, cut in 2.5 cm/1 inch lengths
30 ml/2 tbsp water
2 tsp cornflour
1 egg yolk
2 ripe bananas, mashed
liquid sweetener, to taste

Optional topping:
1 egg white
few drops fresh lemon juice
15 ml/1 tbsp fructose
½ tsp arrowroot

Heat the oven to 200°C/400°F/gas 6.

Roll out the pastry and use to line a 19 cm/7½ inch flan tin. Chill for 15–20 minutes. Then bake blind in the oven for 15 minutes. Remove the baking beans and bake for a further 5 minutes. Leave to go cold.

Put the rhubarb with half the water in a saucepan and simmer until just tender. Mix together the cornflour, remaining water and egg yolk and stir into the rhubarb. Bring to the boil, stirring all the time. Lower the heat and simmer until thickened. Leave to go cold, stirring from time to time. When cold, add the bananas and liquid sweetener, to taste. Spoon into the flan case and serve or cover with the topping.

To make optional topping, whisk the egg white until stiff, then whisk in remaining ingredients. Pipe or spoon decoratively on top of the flan and brown under the grill.

Lemon mallow tart ★

Serves 8

Each serving: 180 kcal/757 kJ, 10 g carbohydrate, 1 g fibre, 4 g protein, 12 g fat

½ quantity Basic wholemeal pastry (see page 43)
15 ml/1 tbsp cornflour
100 ml/4 fl oz skimmed milk
2 eggs, separated
finely grated rind and juice of 2 lemons
40 g/1½ oz fructose
50 g/2 oz polyunsaturated margarine
1 tsp arrowroot

Rhubarb and banana tart (*top*); Blackcurrant and apple crunch (*bottom*, see page 59)
Overleaf: Raspberry lattice flan (*top left*, see page 66); Pumpernickel fool (*top right*, see page 104); Kiwi cups (*bottom left*, see page 91); Bumble bees (*bottom right*, see page 56)

Heat the oven to 200°C/400°F/gas 6.

Roll out the pastry and use to line a 19 cm/7½ inch flan tin. Chill for 15–20 minutes. Then bake blind in the oven for 15 minutes. Remove the baking beans and return to the oven for a further 5 minutes. Leave to go cold.

In a saucepan, mix the cornflour with the milk and egg yolks. Stir in the lemon rind and juice, 15 g/½ oz of the fructose, and the margarine. Cook, stirring, over gentle heat until thickened. Remove from the heat and leave to go cold. Spread the lemon filling over the base of the pastry case.

Put the egg whites in a bowl and whisk until stiff. Whisk in the remaining fructose, and the arrowroot, a little at a time. Using a medium star nozzle, pipe the topping over the lemon filling. Brown under a medium grill until golden.

FLANS

Fruit flan

Serves 8

Each serving: 159 kcal/666 kJ, 15 g carbohydrate, 1 g fibre, 4 g protein, 6 g fat

½ quantity Basic wholemeal pastry (see page 43)
1 quantity Pastry cream with bay leaf flavouring (see page 110)
411 g/14½ oz can fruit salad, in fruit juice
½ tsp arrowroot

Heat the oven to 200°C/400°F/gas 6.

Roll out the pastry and use to line a 20 cm/8 inch flan tin. Chill for 15–20 minutes. Bake blind for 20 minutes. Leave to cool. When cold spread the base with the pastry cream. Drain the fruit salad, reserving the juice, and arrange the fruit over the pastry cream. Simmer the fruit juice in a saucepan until reduced by half. Whisk in the arrowroot and cook, stirring, until thickened. Cool slightly then brush over the fruit to glaze. Serve on the day of assembling.

Tropical fruit flan

Serves 8

Each serving: 125 kcal/527 kJ, 10 g carbohydrate, 1 g fibre, 7 g protein, 5 g fat

2 eggs, separated
30 ml/2 tbsp hot water
25 g/1 oz Pear and apple spread (see page 28)

→

Tropical fruit flan

25 g/1 oz polyunsaturated margarine, plus extra for greasing
50 g/2 oz wholemeal flour
1 tsp baking powder

Filling:
grated rind of 1 lemon
225 g/8 oz cottage cheese, sieved
liquid sweetener, to taste
285 g/10½ oz can guava halves in fruit juice, drained, juice reserved
½ paw paw, peeled, seeded and sliced
1 kiwi fruit, peeled and sliced
½ tsp arrowroot

Heat the oven to 190°C/375°F/gas 5 and lightly grease a 20 cm/8 inch sponge flan tin. Put the egg yolks in a bowl and whisk until thick and creamy. Whisk in the hot water and pear and apple spread. Beat in the margarine, then the flour and baking powder.

In another bowl, whisk the egg whites until stiff, then fold into the flour mixture. Pour the mixture into the flan tin. Bake for 10 minutes until risen and firm to the touch. Cool on a wire tray.

To make the filling, mix the lemon rind with the cottage cheese and add liquid sweetener, to taste. Spread the mixture over the cooled flan, then arrange the fruit on top. Pour the reserved juice into a saucepan and boil until reduced by half. Whisk in the arrowroot and cook, stirring until thickened. Lightly brush the fruit and flan case with this mixture to glaze.

Raspberry lattice flan ★ ★

Serves 10 **see photograph, page 62**

Each serving: 120 kcal/505 kJ, 15 g carbohydrate, 4 g fibre, 2 g protein, 6 g fat

½ quantity of Basic wholemeal pastry (see page 43)
liquid sweetener, to taste
25 g/1 oz polyunsaturated margarine

Filling:
1 tsp ground cinnamon
45 ml/3 tbsp semolina
411 g/14½ oz can raspberries in fruit juice

Topping:
1 egg white
15 ml/1 tbsp fructose
few drops lemon juice

Heat the oven to 200°C/400°F/gas 6.

Roll out the pastry and line a 19 cm/7½ inch flan tin. Chill for 15–20 minutes. Then bake blind for 15 minutes. Remove the baking beans and bake for a further 5 minutes. Leave to cool. Reduce the oven to 180°C/350°F/gas 4.

To make the filling, add the cinnamon and semolina to the raspberries in a saucepan, bring to boil and simmer for 5 minutes. Cool, then add liquid sweetener, to taste, and the margarine. Spread the raspberry mixture in the flan case.

To make the topping, whisk the egg white in a bowl until stiff. Whisk in the fructose a little at a time, and the lemon juice. Using a medium star nozzle, pipe the egg white in a lattice effect on top of the flan. Return to the oven for 7–8 minutes to brown. Serve just warm or cold.

Individual apple pizzas

Serves 4
Each pizza: 204 kcal/857 kJ, 40 g carbohydrate, 5 g fibre, 4 g protein, 5 g fat

½ quantity Quick bread pastry dough (see page 44)
4 tsp polyunsaturated margarine
2 large dessert apples, quartered, cored and thinly sliced
60 ml/4 tbsp sugar-free jam or marmalade, sieved

Heat the oven to 200°C/400°F/gas 6. Divide the dough into four equal portions. Knead each one lightly on a floured surface, then roll out to a round about 12–15 cm/5–6 inch in diameter. Spread each round with a little margarine and place on a non-stick baking sheet. Make a cartwheel of apple slices on top of each round of dough. Place 15 ml/1 tbsp of jam or marmalade in the centre of each cartwheel.

Bake for about 20 minutes until the dough is crisp and the apple tender. Using a knife, spread the remaining jam or marmalade evenly over the apples to glaze. Serve warm.

Warm peach cartwheel

Serves 4
Each serving: 237 kcal/997 kJ, 40 g carbohydrate, 8 g fibre, 6 g protein, 6 g fat

115 g/4 oz wholemeal flour
1 tsp baking powder
½ tsp ground mixed spice
pinch of salt
25 g/1 oz polyunsaturated margarine, plus extra for greasing
411 g/14½ oz can peach slices in fruit juice, drained and juice reserved
30 ml/2 tbsp thick set plain yoghurt
ground cinnamon

Heat the oven to 200°C/400°F/gas 6 and lightly grease a baking tray. Mix together the flour, baking powder, mixed spice and salt in a bowl. Rub in the margarine. Stir in sufficient peach juice to mix to a firm dough. On a lightly floured surface, knead the dough gently and roll out to a 20 cm/8 inch round.

Place the round on the baking tray. Crimp the edges, and arrange the peach slices in a pattern on top. Dot with yoghurt and sprinkle with cinnamon. Bake for 20–25 minutes. Transfer to a serving plate and serve warm in wedges.

Fruit and cheese slice ★ ★

Makes 16 pieces

Each piece: 120 kcal/504 kJ, 15 g carbohydrate, 1 g fibre, 6 g protein, 3 g fat

15 g/½ oz fresh yeast (or 7 g/¼ oz dried yeast)
90 ml/6 tbsp lukewarm skimmed milk
15 ml/1 tbsp fructose
225 g/8 oz plain flour
pinch of salt
25 g/1 oz polyunsaturated margarine, plus extra for greasing
½ egg, beaten

Topping:
350 g/12 oz low-fat soft cheese
1½ eggs, beaten
15 ml/1 tbsp cornflour
grated rind of ½ lemon
25 g/1 oz fructose
2 × 411 g/14½ oz cans fruit cocktail in fruit juice, drained

Lightly grease a 33 × 23 cm/13 × 9 inch Swiss roll tin. Cream the yeast with the milk and fructose in a small bowl and leave in a warm place for about 15 minutes or until frothy.

Sift the flour and salt into a bowl and rub in the margarine. Add the yeast mixture and beaten egg and mix to a dough. Knead the dough on a lightly floured surface for 5 minutes. Return the dough to a lightly oiled bowl, cover with oiled polythene, and leave in a warm place for 40–60 minutes or until risen and doubled in size. Heat the oven to 220°C/425°F/gas 7.

Meanwhile make the topping. Mix together the cheese, eggs, cornflour, lemon rind and fructose.

Punch down the dough, knead lightly and roll out to fit the base of the prepared tin. Spread the cheese mixture on top and sprinkle with the fruit cocktail.

Bake for 20–25 minutes. Allow to cool slightly then cut in slices and serve warm.

PUDDINGS

BAKED PUDDINGS

Strawberry Clafoutis ★ ★

Serves 8

Each serving: 130 kcal/548 kJ, 10 g carbohydrate, 2 g fibre, 5 g protein, 6 g fat

40 g/1½ oz polyunsaturated margarine, plus extra for greasing
3 eggs
25 g/1 oz fructose
65 g/2½ oz wholemeal flour
pinch of salt
300 ml/½ pt skimmed milk
225 g/8 oz strawberries
30 ml/2 tbsp sugar-free strawberry jam, warmed and sieved

Heat the oven to 200°C/400°F/gas 6 and lightly grease a 23 cm/9 inch pottery flan dish. Put the eggs and fructose in a bowl and whisk together. Put the flour and salt in another bowl. Heat the milk and pour over the flour. Beat to a smooth mixture. Add the eggs and fructose and mix well. Pour the batter into the flan dish and arrange the strawberries on top.

Bake for about 30 minutes, until risen and golden. Brush the top of the clafoutis with the strawberry jam and serve at once.

David's date pudding ★ ★ ★

Serves 6
Each serving: 208 kcal/872 kJ, 40 g carbohydrate, 7 g fibre, 6 g protein, 4 g fat

225 g/8 oz stoned dates
300 ml/½ pt water
grated rind of 1 orange
175 g/6 oz wholemeal breadcrumbs
300–350 ml/10–12 fl oz skimmed milk
25 g/1 oz desiccated coconut or long thread coconut
15 ml/1 tbsp sesame or sunflower seeds or 1 tsp poppy seeds

Heat the oven to 190°C/375°F/gas 5 and grease a 900 ml/1½ pt ovenproof serving dish. Place the dates in a saucepan with the water and orange rind. Simmer gently for about 15 minutes and mash to a soft purée. Spread the date purée over the base of the prepared dish and cover with the breadcrumbs. Pour over enough of the milk until it just starts to show through the crumbs. Sprinkle with the coconut and seeds and bake for about 45 minutes until the surface is crisp and golden. Serve warm.

Apple and almond pudding ★

Serves 4
Each serving: 248 kcal/1041 kJ, 10 g carbohydrate, 4 g fibre, 7 g protein, 16 g fat

30 ml/2 tbsp polyunsaturated margarine, plus extra for greasing
30 ml/2 tbsp wholemeal flour
100 ml/4 fl oz skimmed milk
40 g/1½ oz fructose
2 eggs, separated
¼ tsp almond essence
50 g/2 oz blanched almonds, toasted and chopped
1 medium cooking apple (about 175 g/6 oz), peeled, cored and coarsely grated

→

Heat the oven to 180°C/350°F/gas 4 and lightly grease a 750 ml/ 1¼ pt ovenproof serving dish. Melt the margarine in a saucepan. Stir in the flour and cook, stirring, for 1 minute. Stir in the milk and bring to the boil. Remove from the heat. Stir in the fructose, egg yolks and almond essence and beat well. Stir in the almonds and grated apple. Stiffly whisk the egg whites and fold through the almond apple mixture.

Pour into the dish and bake for about 40 minutes until risen and firm to the touch. Serve warm.

Sweet potato pudding ★

Serves 8

Each serving: 194 kcal/813 kJ, 20 g carbohydrate, 3 g fibre, 4 g protein, 10 g fat

2 medium sweet potatoes (about 500 g/ 1 lb 2 oz), peeled and roughly chopped
50 g/2 oz polyunsaturated margarine, plus extra for greasing
50 g/2 oz raisins, minced
50 g/2 oz sugar-free muesli
grated rind and juice of ½ orange
grated rind and juice of ½ lemon
¼ tsp ground nutmeg
2 eggs, separated
50 g/2 oz shelled walnuts, chopped

Lightly grease a 900 ml/1½ pt ovenproof serving dish. Steam or boil the sweet potatoes for about 20 minutes until tender. Drain well and mash. Beat in all the remaining ingredients, except the egg whites and walnuts. Heat the oven to 170°C/325°F/gas 3.

Stiffly whisk the egg whites and fold into the sweet potato mixture. Spoon the mixture into the prepared dish. Sprinkle with the chopped walnuts and bake for about 45 minutes until just firm to the touch.

Baked chocolate provençale ★ ★

Serves 4

Each serving: 160 kcal/674 kJ, 10 g carbohydrate, 1 g fibre, 7 g protein, 7 g fat

150 ml/¼ pt skimmed milk
15 ml/1 tbsp polyunsaturated margarine, plus extra for greasing
25 g/1 oz cocoa or carob powder
40 g/1½ oz fructose
2 eggs, separated
50 g/2 oz fresh wholemeal breadcrumbs

Heat the oven to 180°C/350°F/gas 4 and lightly grease a 750 ml/ 1¼ pt ovenproof serving dish. Place the milk, margarine, cocoa or carob powder and fructose in a saucepan. Heat gently and mix well. Remove from the heat and stir in the egg yolks and then the breadcrumbs. Leave to cool. Stiffly whisk the egg whites and fold into the chocolate mixture until evenly incorporated.

Transfer to the dish and bake for 25–30 minutes until risen and just firm to the touch. Serve warm with Pouring custard (see page 112).

Rice pudding ⊠ ⊠

Serves 4

Each serving: 220 kcal/926 kJ, 30 g carbohydrate, 1 g fibre, 10 g protein, 7 g fat

115 g/4 oz short-grain brown rice, washed
900 ml/1½ pt skimmed milk
2 thinly pared twists of lemon or orange rind
30 ml/2 tbsp polyunsaturated margarine
pinch of ground nutmeg
liquid sweetener, to taste

Place the rice in a saucepan with the remaining ingredients, except the sweetener, and bring to the boil. Reduce the heat, cover the pan and simmer, stirring occasionally for about 1 hour, until tender. Remove the lemon or orange rind and add sweetener to taste. If you like, transfer to a heatproof serving dish and brown under the grill for several minutes.

Variation: About 10 minutes from the end of cooking time, stir in 50–75 g/2–3 oz chopped dates or figs, sultanas or raisins instead of the sweetener.

Poppy seed pudding ⊠ ⊠

Serves 4

Each serving: (without jam) 122 kcal/513 kJ, 20 g carbohydrate, neg fibre, 8 g protein, 2 g fat
(With jam) 159 kcal/668 kJ, 30 g carbohydrate, 1 g fibre, 8 g protein, 2 g fat

2 tsp poppy seeds
600 ml/1 pt skimmed milk
60 ml/4 tbsp ground rice
1 egg, beaten
liquid sweetener, to taste
squeeze of lemon juice
60 ml/4 tbsp sugar-free jam (optional)

Place the poppy seeds in a heavy-based saucepan and cook over medium heat until they start to jump. Cool the pan slightly before adding the milk and stirring in the ground rice. Simmer, stirring frequently, for about 5 minutes, until thickened. Remove from the heat and beat in the egg. Stir in liquid sweetener and lemon juice to taste. Serve at once, with a spoonful of sugar-free jam, if wished.

STEAMED PUDDINGS

Steamed chocolate chip pudding ★

Serves 4
Each serving: 375 kcal/1574 kJ, 30 g carbohydrate, 3 g fibre, 8 g protein, 20 g fat

50 g/2 oz polyunsaturated margarine, plus extra for greasing
50 g/2 oz fructose
2 eggs
115 g/4 oz wholemeal flour
pinch of salt
1 tsp baking powder
50 g/2 oz chocolate, cut in small pieces
25 g/1 oz shelled walnuts, chopped

Lightly grease a 900 ml/1½ pt pudding basin. Place all the ingredients in a bowl and beat well with a wooden spoon for 1–2 minutes until evenly mixed. Transfer the mixture to the pudding basin. Cover the basin with a piece of greased foil with a pleat in it to allow for expansion. Tie down securely with string.

Place the basin in a large saucepan. Pour in boiling water to come at least half-way up the sides of the basin. Cover with a lid and simmer gently for about 1¾ hours until the pudding has risen and is firm to the touch. Add more boiling water if necessary. Unmould the pudding on to a serving plate and serve at once with Pouring custard (see page 112).

Cottage cheese and lemon dumplings with peach sauce ★

Serves 4
Each serving: 332 kcal/1393 kJ, 25 g carbohydrate, 7 g fibre, 10 g protein, 23 g fat

50 g/2 oz wholemeal breadcrumbs
25 g/1 oz polyunsaturated margarine
1 egg, beaten
50 g/2 oz cottage cheese
25 g/1 oz self-raising flour
pinch of salt
grated rind of ½ lemon
50 g/2 oz ground almonds
liquid sweetener, to taste
50 g/2 oz desiccated coconut, toasted
411 g/14½ oz can peach slices in fruit juice, puréed

Cottage cheese and lemon dumplings with peach sauce (*top*); Steamed chocolate chip pudding with Pouring custard (*bottom*); Pouring custard (see page 112)

Put the first nine ingredients into a bowl and beat until well mixed. Shape the mixture into twelve even-sized ovals with two spoons. Arrange well apart in a steamer and steam for about 10 minutes until firm to the touch. Roll immediately in the toasted coconut and serve at once with the peach purée, either warm or cold.

BREAD PUDDINGS

Sunshine bread pudding ★ ★

Serves 6

Each serving: 180 kcal/756 kJ, 20 g carbohydrate, 3 g fibre, 7 g protein, 8 g fat

40 g/1½ oz polyunsaturated margarine
4 large thin slices wholemeal bread
60 ml/4 tbsp sugar-free orange marmalade
450 ml/¾ pt skimmed milk
2 eggs, beaten
½ tsp vanilla essence
freshly ground nutmeg

Use 15 g/½ oz margarine to grease a 1.1 litre/2 pt ovenproof serving dish. Spread the bread evenly with the remaining margarine and then with the marmalade. Cut each slice into four triangles. Arrange the bread in the dish.

Heat the milk to just below boiling point. Beat in the eggs and vanilla and pour over the bread slices. Leave to soak for 30 minutes. Heat the oven to 180°C/350°F/gas 4.

Place the dish in a roasting tin. Pour in enough hot water to come half-way up the sides of the dish. Sprinkle with nutmeg and bake for about 45 minutes until set and crisp on top.

Spiced bread pudding ★ ★

Serves 4

Each serving: 355 kcal/1490 kJ, 45 g carbohydrate, 7 g fibre, 12 g protein, 15 g fat

225 g/8 oz wholemeal bread, cubed
450 ml/¾ pt skimmed milk
50 g/2 oz polyunsaturated margarine, plus extra for greasing
50 g/2 oz each sultanas and currants
1 tsp ground ginger
1 tsp ground cinnamon
½ tsp ground nutmeg
2 eggs, beaten
a little powdered sweetener to sprinkle (optional)

→

Summer pudding (see page 77)

Heat the oven to 180°C/350°F/gas 4 and grease a 28 × 18 cm/ 11 × 7 inch ovenproof baking dish. Place the bread in a bowl. Bring the milk to the boil, stir in the margarine and pour over the bread. Leave to soak for 15 minutes. Add the remaining ingredients and beat well. Transfer to the baking dish and bake for 45 minutes until golden, and firm to the touch.

Serve cut in squares and sprinkled with sweetener, if wished. Any leftover pudding may be eaten cold.

MOULDED PUDDINGS

Savarin ★ ★

Serves 8

Each serving: 152 kcal/639 kJ, 20 g carbohydrate, 2 g fibre, 6 g protein, 7 g fat

15 g/½ oz fresh yeast
45 ml/3 tbsp lukewarm skimmed milk
50 g/2 oz wholemeal flour
50 g/2 oz strong plain flour
pinch of salt
15 g/½ oz fructose
2 medium-sized eggs, beaten
50 g/2 oz polyunsaturated margarine, plus extra for greasing
411 g/14½ oz can pears (or other fruit), in fruit juice
30 ml/2 tbsp sugar-free apricot jam, warmed and sieved
115 g/4 oz fresh strawberries, hulled and halved

Lightly grease an 18 cm/7 inch ring mould. Crumble the yeast into a bowl. Stir in the milk and dissolve the yeast. Add 25 g/1 oz of the wholemeal flour and blend together until smooth. Leave in a warm place for about 20 minutes or until frothy.

Stir in the remaining flours, salt, fructose, eggs and margarine. Beat together for 3–4 minutes. Spoon the mixture into the prepared mould. Cover with greased polythene and return to a warm place for 30–40 minutes or until the dough has almost risen to the top of the mould. Heat the oven to 200°C/400°F/gas 6. When risen remove the polythene and bake for 15–20 minutes until the savarin is golden brown in colour.

Invert the savarin on to a wire tray. Cool slightly and prick all over with a fine skewer. Drain the pears. Put the juice in a saucepan and boil until reduced to 100 ml/4 fl oz. Pour the reduced juice over the savarin. Brush the jam over the surface of the savarin. Fill the centre of the savarin with the drained pears and the strawberries, reserving about twelve to fourteen strawberries for decoration.

Apricot rice ring with raspberry sauce

Serves 4 ★ ★ ★

Each serving: 218 kcal/918 kJ, 45 g carbohydrate, 14 g fibre, 7 g protein, 2 g fat

75 g/3 oz pudding rice
300 ml/½ pt skimmed milk
411 g/14½ oz can apricot halves in fruit juice, drained and juice reserved
15 ml/1 tbsp custard powder
1 egg yolk
liquid sweetener, to taste

Sauce:
225 g/8 oz raspberries
30 ml/2 tbsp sugar-free raspberry jam, or liquid sweetener to taste

Wash the rice well. Put the rice and milk in a saucepan and simmer for about 25 minutes until the rice is tender and all the milk has been absorbed.

Mix the apricot juice with the custard powder in a saucepan and simmer gently until thickened. Immediately stir in the rice and egg yolk. Beat well, then leave to cool. Stir in the sweetener to taste. Press the rice mixture into a 450 ml/¾ pt mould or spoon into four individual serving dishes. Chill until required.

To make the sauce, purée the raspberries then pass them through a sieve to remove the seeds. Stir in the jam or sweetener to taste. Unmould the rice ring on to a serving plate and decorate with the apricot halves. Spoon a little raspberry sauce over the top and hand the remaining sauce separately.

Summer pudding ★ ★ ★

Serves 8 **see photograph, page 74**

Each serving: 80 kcal/336 kJ, 15 g carbohydrate, 6 g fibre, 3 g protein, 1 g fat

8 large slices wholemeal bread, crusts removed
700 g/1½ lb mixed summer fruits (e.g. raspberries, strawberries, redcurrants and cherries)
60 ml/4 tbsp low-calorie lemon and lime drink
1 tsp gelatine
liquid sweetener, to taste
reserve 1 or 2 pieces of fruit for garnish

Use about 7 slices of the bread to line the base and sides of a 1.1 litre/2 pt pudding basin.

In a large saucepan, combine the fruits and lemon and lime drink. Simmer gently for about 5 minutes until tender. Spoon the fruit into the prepared basin, reserving the juice in the pan. Sprinkle the gelatine over the juice in the pan and heat gently to dissolve. Cool, then add the liquid sweetener to taste. Pour the juice over the fruit in the basin. Cover the fruit with the remaining bread, cutting to shape as required. Cover loosely with cling film or greaseproof paper and weight down. Chill for several hours, or overnight. Unmould on to a serving dish and decorate with reserved fruit.

CHEESECAKES AND PANCAKES

CHEESECAKES

Quick pineapple cheesecake ★ ★

Serves 8 **see photograph, page 84**

Each serving: 195 kcal/820 kJ, 15 g carbohydrate, 3 g fibre, 12 g protein, 9 g fat

Base:
50 g/2 oz desiccated coconut
50 g/2 oz wheatgerm
25 g/1 oz polyunsaturated margarine, melted
30 ml/2 tbsp sugar-free apricot jam, or marmalade

Filling:
225 g/8 oz can pineapple in fruit juice
450 g/1 lb cottage cheese
25 g/1 oz fructose
½ tsp lemon juice
15 g/½ oz gelatine (or 15 ml/1 tbsp)

Topping:
225 g/8 oz can pineapple in fruit juice
1 tsp arrowroot
scented geranium leaves, to decorate

Line the base and sides of an 18 cm/7 inch loose-bottomed cake tin with greaseproof paper.

Toast the coconut and wheatgerm in a non-stick frying pan over a gentle heat. Mix together with the margarine and jam or marmalade and press into the base of the prepared tin. Put into the refrigerator to chill.

To make the filling, drain the pineapple and reserve the juice. Place the pineapple, cheese, fructose and lemon juice in a food processor, or blender, and purée until smooth. Dissolve the gelatine in the reserved juice, then stir into the cheese mixture. Spoon the mixture into the cake tin and return to the refrigerator until set.

To make the topping, drain the pineapple and put the juice into a saucepan. Stir in the arrowroot and bring to the boil, stirring. Cook gently until thickened. Remove from the heat and allow the glaze to cool. Transfer the cheesecake to a serving dish. Arrange the pineapple pieces around the outside edge and brush with glaze; then spoon the remaining glaze into the centre. Chill until required. Decorate with scented geranium leaves and serve.

Orange cheesecake

Serves 6

Each serving: 204 kcal/858 kJ, 20 g carbohydrate, 2 g fibre, 10 g protein, 10 g fat

Base:
50 g/2 oz toasted breadcrumbs
25 g/1 oz shelled walnuts or hazelnuts, finely chopped
25 g/1 oz chocolate
25 g/1 oz polyunsaturated margarine, plus extra for greasing

Topping:
225 g/8 oz low-fat soft cheese
100 ml/4 fl oz low-fat plain yoghurt
2 eggs, separated
25 g/1 oz flour
50 g/2 oz fructose
2 large oranges

Mix together the breadcrumbs and walnuts or hazelnuts. In a saucepan, melt the chocolate and margarine and stir into the breadcrumb mixture. Press on to the base of a lightly greased 20 cm/8 inch spring release cake tin and chill.

To make the topping, beat together the cheese, yoghurt, egg yolks, flour, fructose and grated rind of 1 orange. Gently whisk the egg whites and fold into the mixture. Pour the mixture into the cake tin and bake at 180°C/350°F/gas 4 for 25–30 minutes until set. Leave to go cold, then remove from the tin.

Peel the rind and pith from the oranges and carefully remove each orange segment. Use to decorate the cheesecake.

Gooseberry cheesecake

Serves 12

Each serving: 113 kcal/473 kJ, 10 g carbohydrate, 1 g fibre, 6 g protein, 6 g fat

Base:
115 g/4 oz digestive biscuits, crushed
50 g/2 oz polyunsaturated margarine, plus extra for greasing

Topping:
30 ml/2 tbsp custard powder
300 ml/½ pt skimmed milk
225 g/8 oz gooseberries, topped and tailed
30 ml/2 tbsp water
15 g/½ oz gelatine (or 15 ml/1 tbsp)
225 g/8 oz cottage cheese, sieved
liquid sweetener, to taste
1 egg white

Mix together the digestive biscuits and margarine and press into the base of an 18 cm/7 inch lightly greased loose-bottomed (or spring release) cake tin, and chill.

To make the topping, mix the custard powder with a little milk in a bowl. Heat the remaining milk, and pour on to the custard powder. Return to the pan and cook, stirring, until thickened. Cool, stirring occasionally to prevent a skin forming.

Put the gooseberries with the water in a saucepan and cook over gentle heat until soft. Drain the gooseberries and pour the juice into a small saucepan. Sprinkle the gelatine on top of the gooseberry juice and dissolve over gentle heat.

Combine the custard, gooseberries, gelatine and cottage cheese, and beat well. Cool, then add liquid sweetener to taste.

Whisk the egg white until stiff then fold into the gooseberry mixture. Pour the mixture on to the chilled base. Return to the refrigerator until set. Unmould on to a serving plate.

Strawberry cheesecake ★ ★

Serves 12

Each serving: 83 kcal/349 kJ, 10 g carbohydrate, 1 g fibre, 3 g protein, 4 g fat

Base:
50 g/2 oz wholemeal flour
50 g/2 oz rolled oats
50 g/2 oz polyunsaturated margarine, plus extra for greasing
15 ml/1 tbsp sugar-free strawberry jam

Topping:
225 g/8 oz strawberries
15 g/½ oz gelatine (or 15 ml/1 tbsp)
45 ml/3 tbsp water
175 g/6 oz curd cheese
150 ml/¼ pt Greek strained yoghurt
liquid sweetener, to taste
1 egg white
12 strawberries, to decorate

Heat the oven to 200°C/400°F/gas 6.

Mix together the flour, oats, margarine and jam and press into the bottom of an 18 cm/7 inch lightly greased loose-bottomed cake tin. Bake for 10 minutes. Set aside to cool while preparing the filling.

Crush the strawberries in a bowl. Put the gelatine and water in a small saucepan and dissolve over very low heat. Add the gelatine to the crushed strawberries and mix in the curd cheese, yoghurt and liquid sweetener, to taste.

Whisk the egg white until stiff and fold into the strawberry mixture. Pour the mixture over the prepared base. Chill for several hours, then remove from the tin and decorate with the reserved strawberries.

PANCAKES

Pancake batter ★ ★ ★

Makes 8

Each pancake without filling: 64 kcal/270 kJ, 10 g carbohydrate, 1 g fibre, 4 g protein, 2 g fat

50 g/2 oz wholemeal flour
pinch of salt (optional)
1 egg
65 ml/2½ fl oz soda water
65 ml/2½ fl oz skimmed milk
a little polyunsaturated oil, for frying (optional)

In a bowl, whisk together the flour, salt, egg, soda water and milk to make a smooth batter. Alternatively, process all the ingredients in a blender or food processor.

To cook the pancakes, heat a non-stick 15 cm/6 inch frying pan until very hot. Pour in 15 ml/1 tbsp of the batter and tilt the pan so that the batter runs all over the base. After about 30 seconds when the bottom of the pancake is cooked, flip it over and cook the other side. Transfer the pancake to a plate and cook the other pancakes in the same manner. If you are using a traditional frying pan, brush the base lightly with oil before frying each pancake.

Spicy apple filling ★ ★

Serves 8

Each serving: 126 kcal/529 kJ, 10 g carbohydrate, 1 g fibre, 8 g protein, 5 g fat

225 g/8 oz cottage cheese
50 g/2 oz raisins
1 dessert apple, cored and finely chopped
1 tsp ground cinnamon
30 ml/2 tbsp polyunsaturated margarine or low-fat spread
ground cinnamon, to sprinkle

Method (as for Tropical fruit filling).

Tropical fruit filling ★ ★

Serves 8

Each serving: 121 kcal/508 kJ, 15 g carbohydrate, 3 g fibre, 4 g protein, 6 g fat

115 g/4 oz cottage cheese
115 g/4 oz grapes, halved or quartered and pips removed
25 g/1 oz toasted desiccated coconut
2 bananas, chopped
30 ml/2 tbsp polyunsaturated margarine or low-fat spread

Combine all the ingredients for the filling of your choice and divide between the pancakes. Fold the edges in to make neat envelopes. Place the stuffed pancakes in a heatproof serving dish in a single layer. Spread with a little polyunsaturated margarine or low-fat spread and sprinkle with cinnamon, if using. Heat through under a medium grill for 5–10 minutes until crisp on the surface. Serve at once.

Banana pancakes ★ ★

Makes 8

Each pancake: 67 kcal/283 kJ, 10 g carbohydrate, 1 g fibre, 2 g protein, 3 g fat

45 ml/3 tbsp wholemeal flour
pinch of salt
90 ml/6 tbsp skimmed milk
1 egg
2 ripe bananas, chopped
25 g/1 oz polyunsaturated margarine
sugar-free jam, to serve

Place the flour, salt, skimmed milk, egg and bananas in a food processor or blender and process until smooth.

Heat a little of the margarine in a 15 cm/6 inch frying pan. When very hot, pour in one-eighth of the batter. Tilt the pan so that the batter covers the base. Cook for about 30 seconds or until the bottom is golden. Turn the pancake over and cook the other side. Transfer to a plate and keep warm while you make the remaining pancakes. Serve at once with a little jam.

Raspberry omelette ★

Serves 2

Each serving: 178 kcal/746 kJ, 10 g carbohydrate, 5 g fibre, 9 g protein, 12 g fat

25 g/1 oz wholemeal breadcrumbs
60 ml/4 tbsp skimmed milk
2 eggs
½ tsp vanilla essence
liquid sweetener, equivalent to 2 tsp sugar
115 g/4 oz fresh raspberries
15 g/½ oz polyunsaturated margarine

Mix the breadcrumbs and milk together in a bowl and leave to soak for 10 minutes. Add the eggs, vanilla essence and liquid sweetener. Purée three-quarters of the raspberries and add liquid sweetener to taste, if wished. Melt the margarine in a small omelette pan. Pour on the egg mixture and, using a fork, work the mixture into the centre as it begins to cook. When almost cooked, place under the grill and brown quickly.

Transfer to a serving plate and pour over the raspberry purée. Decorate with reserved raspberries.

Sesame crusted pear (*top*, see page 88); Banana pancakes (*bottom*)
Overleaf: Watermelon and ginger jelly (*top left*, see page 99); Chocolate fruit cups (*top right*, see page 90); Blueberry islands (*bottom left*, see page 98); Quick pineapple cheesecake (*bottom right*, see page 78)

Prune fritters

★ ★

Serves 4

Each fritter: 298 kcal/1251 kJ, 40 g carbohydrate, 9 g fibre, 4 g protein, 14 g fat

16 prunes, pitted, soaked overnight in boiling water
sunflower oil, for deep-frying
powdered sweetener, to sprinkle (optional)

Batter:
50 g/2 oz rice flour
40 g/1½ oz wholemeal flour
15 g/½ oz semolina
1 tsp baking powder
1 tsp ground cinnamon
150 ml/¼ pt water or skimmed milk

Simmer the prunes in the soaking water for 15 minutes. Leave to go cold in the liquid. Drain and dry on absorbent kitchen paper towels (reserve the juice for another recipe).

Put all the dry ingredients for the batter in a bowl. Beat in sufficient water or milk to make a coating batter. Heat the oil in a deep frying pan to 180°C/350°F. If you do not have a thermometer, drop in a cube of stale bread; if it browns within 1 minute the oil is hot enough. Dip the prunes in the batter, coating them well then deep-fry until crisp and golden. Drain on absorbent kitchen paper towels and serve at once. Sprinkle with powdered sweetener, if wished.

Note: Other bite-size pieces of prepared fresh fruit may be used, such as apple, pineapple or banana.

BAKED, FRESH AND DRIED FRUIT

BAKED FRUIT

Baked apples

★ ★ ★

Serves 4

Each serving: 91 kcal/381 kJ, 20 g carbohydrate, 3 g fibre, 1 g protein, 1 g fat

4 dessert apples
115 g/4 oz Spiced mincemeat (see page 116)
60 ml/4 tbsp water

→

Winter fruit medley (*top*, see page 91); Guava custards with toasted coconut (*bottom*, see page 101)

Heat the oven to 200°C/400°F/gas 6.

Wash and core the apples and make a cut round each circumference. Stand the apples in a baking dish and fill the centres with the mincemeat. Add the water to the dish and bake for 25 minutes, until the apples are tender.

Baked pears ★ ★ ★

Serves 4

Each serving: 128 kcal/538 kJ, 20 g carbohydrate, 3 g fibre, 1 g protein, 3 g fat

4 fairly ripe Conference pears, peeled, halved and cored
60 ml/4 tbsp sugar-free apricot jam
30 ml/2 tbsp flaked almonds
150 ml/¼ pt unsweetened white grape juice or medium-dry white wine

Heat the oven to 180°C/350°F/gas 4. Place the pears in a baking dish and spoon a little jam into the centre of each. Sprinkle with flaked almonds. Pour the grape juice or white wine carefully round the pears and bake for about 20 minutes, until just tender. Serve warm.

Baked apples in pastry cases ★

Serves 4

Each serving: 455 kcal/1909 kJ, 55 g carbohydrate, 8 g fibre, 9 g protein, 24 g fat

4 dessert apples, washed and cored
115 g/4 oz Spiced mincemeat (see page 116)
1 quantity Basic wholemeal pastry (see page 43)
1 egg, beaten

Heat the oven to 200°C/400°F/gas 6. Make a cut round the circumference of each apple. Fill the centres with the mincemeat.

Cut the pastry into four. Roll out each piece of pastry thinly and stamp out a circle large enough to enclose each apple. Place an apple in the middle of the pastry circle. Lift and work the pastry to enclose the apple completely. Put the apples on a non-stick baking sheet. Use any trimmings to cut out some leaves and stalks for decoration; brush the pastry-covered apples with water and press the pastry leaves and stalks on to the apples.

Brush with beaten egg and bake for 25 minutes, until the apples are tender and the pastry crisp and golden.

Sesame crusted pears ★ ★

Serves 4 see photograph, page 83

Each pear: 257 kcal/1079 kJ, 30 g carbohydrate, 7 g fibre, 8 g protein, 11 g fat

4 medium-sized ripe dessert pears (eg. Williams)
½ quantity Almond paste (see page 111)
½ quantity Quick bread dough (see page 44)
1 egg white, beaten
30 ml/2 tbsp sesame seeds

Heat the oven to 200°C/400°F/gas 6. Wash and dry the pears, leaving the stalks in place. Cut a small slice from the base of each pear so that they stand upright. Using a small sharp knife, remove the core starting from the base so that the pears remain whole.

Roll the almond paste into four 'barrel' shapes, and press one piece into each pear to fill the cored area. Divide the dough into four equal pieces. Roll each piece on a lightly floured surface until it is large enough to enclose a pear completely. Brush the edges of the dough with egg white and carefully encase each pear, pressing the edges together to seal. Reserve trimmings to make eight leaves. Put the pears on a non-stick baking sheet. Brush the outside of each covered pear with egg white and sprinkle with the sesame seeds. Attach leaves and bake for about 30 minutes until golden and tender when tested with a skewer.

Sautéed bananas ★ ★

Serves 4
Each serving: 169 kcal/710 kJ, 25 g carbohydrate, 4 g fibre, 2 g protein, 7 g fat

25 g/1 oz polyunsaturated margarine
4 bananas, thickly sliced
120 ml/8 tbsp orange juice
25 g/1 oz raisins or sultanas
¼ tsp ground cinnamon
30 ml/2 tbsp toasted chopped hazelnuts or pistachio nuts

Melt the margarine in a large non-stick frying pan and sauté the bananas until golden on both sides. Add the orange juice, raisins or sultanas and cinnamon. Cover and simmer for 5 minutes until the bananas are just tender. Sprinkle with chopped nuts and serve at once.

FRESH FRUIT

Fresh fruit platter

One of the nicest desserts to serve when on a diet is a fresh fruit platter – a beautiful arrangement of prepared fruit served on a plate (glass or china), rather than a fruit salad served in a syrup.

The choice of fruits is very important – choose interesting fruits with a good combination of flavours and colours, or keep to one colour for a dramatic effect. For example, for a platter of yellow fruit, choose mango, paw paw, oranges, apricots and yellow plums. To prepare the mango, hold it upright on a plate. Using a sharp knife, and keeping it as close to the central stone as possible, cut downwards to slice off one 'cheek'. Then turn the fruit around and slice off the other 'cheek'. Cut the cheeks in half, then peel. Cube or cut the flesh in strips. Cut the flesh off the stone. Prepare paw paws as you would melon.

Other combinations may include pineapple, strawberries and banana (banana discolours easily so add it at the last moment or dip in lemon juice); or for an all red mixture, use raspberries, strawberries, red plums and cherries.

A little soft cheese or a scoop of sorbet may be added as well. Serve lightly chilled, but not ice-cold.

Sarah's summer salad ⊞ ★ ★ ★

Serves 4

Each serving: 27 kcal/114 kJ, 5 g carbohydrate, 3 g fibre, 1 g protein, 0 g fat

½ medium-sized melon
115 g/4 oz strawberries or raspberries
1 kiwi fruit, peeled and sliced

Remove the seeds from the melon and, using a melon baller, make as many melon balls as possible. Using a spoon, scrape out the remaining melon and purée in a blender. Hull the strawberries and slice or halve, or pick over the raspberries, if using. Place the melon balls and purée in a serving dish. Carefully stir in the strawberries, or raspberries, and the kiwi fruit. Chill until required.

Chocolate fruit cups ★ ★

Serves 4 **see photograph, page 84**

Each serving: 102 kcal/427 kJ, 15 g carbohydrate, 3 g fibre, 1 g protein, 4 g fat

50 g/2 oz chocolate
200 g/7 oz prepared fresh fruit, chopped (e.g. plums, mango, dates, grapefruit, orange, pomegranate, passion fruit)

Break the chocolate into pieces and put in a heatproof bowl. Place the bowl over a pan of very gently simmering water. Stir to melt the chocolate. When melted, brush the chocolate on the inside of four paper cake cases. Apply a thin layer, then place the cases in the freezer for about 10 minutes. Brush the remaining chocolate inside the cases and return to the freezer.

When set hard, remove the paper and divide the prepared fruit between the chocolate cups. Serve immediately.

Kiwi cups ★ ★ ★

Serves 4

see photograph, page 62

Each serving: 75 kcal/316 kJ, 10 g carbohydrate, 3 g fibre, 5 g protein, 1 g fat

4 large firm kiwi fruit
½ quantity Lemon delight (see (page 105)
4 small strawberries, to decorate

Cut a small slice from the stalk end of each kiwi fruit so that they stand upright. Using an apple corer, carefully remove the centre core, and discard. Using a small sharp knife or potato peeler, peel the fruit.

Stand each fruit on a small plate. Spoon the Lemon delight mixture into the centre of each kiwi. Decorate with slices of fresh strawberry and serve at once.

Note: The kiwi fruit and Lemon delight can be prepared well in advance. However they should be filled just before serving.

Redcurrant and raspberry kissel ★ ★ ★

Serves 6

Each serving: 110 kcal/460 kJ, 10 g carbohydrate, 6 g fibre, 1 g protein, 0 g fat

225 g/8 oz fresh or frozen raspberries
225 g/8 oz fresh or frozen redcurrants
300 ml/½ pt water
115 g/4 oz fructose
50 g/2 oz ground rice

Pick over the fruits and place in a saucepan with the water. If frozen, bring slowly to the boil.

Mix the fructose and ground rice in a bowl. Pour on a little of the liquid from the saucepan, stirring all the time. Return this mixture to the saucepan and simmer gently, stirring frequently, for 5 minutes until thickened. Pour into individual ramekin dishes or small glasses and chill until required. If wished, decorate with a sprig of redcurrants and two fresh raspberries.

DRIED FRUIT

Winter fruit medley ★ ★ ★

Serves 8

see photograph, page 86

Each serving: 108 kcal/453 kJ, 25 g carbohydrate, 7 g fibre, 2 g protein, 0 g fat

→

250 g/9 oz pkt dried fruit salad (eg. apricots, apples, prunes, etc)
75 g/3 oz dried figs
600 ml/1 pt boiling water
1 large orange
1 large pink grapefruit
1 pomegranate

Place the dried fruit salad and figs in a large bowl. Cover with the water and leave to soak for at least 12 hours.

Cut the larger pieces of fruit in half, if wished, then transfer the fruits and their juice to a saucepan and bring to the boil. Reduce the heat, cover and simmer for 15 minutes. Remove from the heat and leave to cool.

Peel the orange and grapefruit with a serrated knife, ensuring that all the white pith is removed. Carefully remove each segment from the central membrane. Squeeze the juice from the skin and peelings and add this to the fruit salad with the orange and grapefruit segments.

Cut the pomegranate in half and, using a teaspoon, scoop out all the seeds and juice. Add to the fruit salad. Mix well, then transfer to a serving dish. Chill until required, but do not serve too cold.

Pecan-stuffed prunes ★ ★

Serves 4
Each serving: 170 kcal/714 kJ, 25 g carbohydrate, 10 g fibre, 3 g protein, 8 g fat

24 large prunes (about 225 g/8 oz)
300 ml/½ pt freshly made weak tea
24 pecan or walnut halves
squeeze of lemon juice
few drops of rosewater (optional)

Wash the prunes and place in a shallow dish or roasting pan. Pour the tea over to cover the prunes completely and leave to soak for at least 12 hours. Drain the prunes, reserving the liquid. Using a small sharp knife, remove the prune stones and replace with the pecan or walnut halves. Arrange in a serving dish. Add the lemon juice and rosewater, if using, to the reserved tea liquid and carefully pour over the prunes.

If you prefer a softer texture, place the prunes in a saucepan, cover with the tea, lemon juice and rosewater and simmer gently for 5 minutes. Transfer to a serving dish and leave to go cold.

Winter compote ★ ★ ★

Serves 4
Each serving: 77 kcal/323 kJ, 20 g carbohydrate, 3 g fibre, 1 g protein, 0 g fat

150 ml/¼ pt unsweetened apple juice
2 dessert apples, preferably Cox's orange pippins, cored and thinly sliced
25 g/1 oz stoned dates, finely chopped
2 oranges

Place the apple juice and apple slices in a wide, shallow saucepan and bring to the boil. Reduce the heat, cover and simmer for about 5 minutes, until just tender. Remove from the heat and sprinkle the dates over the apple slices. Cover and leave to one side while you prepare the oranges.

Using a sharp knife, peel the oranges, removing all the white pith with the rind. Carefully remove each segment of orange from the inner membrane. Squeeze the juice from the peelings and the membrane and reserve. Transfer the apples to a serving dish and carefully stir in the orange segments and juice. Cover and chill until required.

SOUFFLÉS, PUFFLES AND MERINGUES

SOUFFLÉS

Chestnut and chocolate soufflé ★ ★

Serves 4

Each serving: 182 kcal/765 kJ, 15 g carbohydrate, 2 g fibre, 5 g protein, 7 g fat

15 ml/1 tbsp cornflour
100 ml/4 fl oz skimmed milk
15 ml/1 tbsp polyunsaturated margarine, plus extra for greasing
2 eggs, separated
15 ml/1 tbsp cocoa powder
50 g/2 oz fructose
½ tsp vanilla essence
115 g/4 oz unsweetened chestnut purée

Heat the oven to 190°C/375°F/gas 5 and grease a 750 ml/1¼ pt soufflé dish.

In a cup, mix the cornflour to a smooth paste with a little of the milk. Bring the remaining milk to the boil in a saucepan. Stir in the cornflour and margarine and simmer, stirring all the time, until thickened. Beat in the egg yolks, cocoa powder, fructose, vanilla essence and chestnut purée until smooth.

Put the egg whites in a bowl and whisk until stiff. Fold the egg whites into the chestnut mixture. Pour the mixture into the soufflé dish. Place the dish in a roasting tin. Pour in enough hot water to come half-way up the sides of the dish. Bake for 40–45 minutes until risen and firm when shaken slightly. Serve at once.

Chilled pineapple and banana soufflé

★ ★ ★

Serves 10

Each serving: 83 kcal/349 kJ, 5 g carbohydrate, 1 g fibre, 6 g protein, 1 g fat

polyunsaturated margarine, for greasing
300 ml/½ pt pineapple purée, made from about 225–350 g/8–12 oz prepared fresh pineapple
2 bananas, mashed
225 g/8 oz skimmed-milk soft cheese
liquid sweetener, to taste
45 ml/3 tbsp water
15 g/½ oz gelatine (or 15 ml/1 tbsp)
3 egg whites
tiny pieces of fresh pineapple and lemon balm or scented geranium leaves, to decorate

Prepare a 750 ml/1¼ pt soufflé dish by tying a double layer of greased greaseproof paper around the dish so that it extends about 7.5 cm/3 inches above the top to form a collar.

Simmer the pineapple purée for about 5 minutes in a covered saucepan. Cool. Mix in the bananas, cheese and liquid sweetener, to taste. Put the water in a saucepan, sprinkle the gelatine on top and heat gently until it dissolves. Stir the gelatine into the pineapple mixture.

Whisk the egg whites until stiff and carefully fold into the pineapple mixture. Pour the mixture into the prepared soufflé dish and leave to set for at least 4 hours in the refrigerator.

Carefully remove the paper collar and decorate with small pieces of fresh pineapple and lemon balm or scented geranium leaves.

PUFFLES

Lemon and pineapple puffle

★

Serves 4

Each serving: 135 kcal/568 kJ, 10 g carbohydrate, neg fibre, 4 g protein, 6 g fat

15 ml/1 tbsp cornflour
100 ml/4 fl oz skimmed milk
15 ml/1 tbsp polyunsaturated margarine, plus extra for greasing
2 eggs, separated
40 g/1½ oz fructose

Sparkling grape jellies (*top*, see page 100); Chilled pineapple and banana soufflé (*bottom*)

115 g/4 oz pineapple, finely chopped (use either fresh or canned in fruit juice, drained)
1 tsp grated lemon rind
30 ml/2 tbsp lemon juice

Heat the oven to 190°C/375°F/gas 5 and lightly grease a 750 ml/ 1¼ pt ovenproof serving dish.

Mix the cornflour to a smooth paste with a little of the milk. Bring the remaining milk to the boil in a saucepan. Stir in the cornflour and margarine and simmer, stirring all the time, until thickened. Beat in the egg yolks, fructose, chopped pineapple, lemon rind and half the lemon juice.

Stiffly whisk the egg whites in a bowl. Whisk in the remaining lemon juice. Fold the egg whites into the custard until evenly combined, then transfer the mixture to the prepared serving dish. Place the dish in a roasting tin. Pour boiling water into the tin to come half-way up the sides of the dish. Bake for about 40 minutes until risen and firm when shaken slightly. Serve at once.

Prune puffle ⊞ ★ ★ ★

Serves 4

Each serving: 58 kcal/244 kJ, 10 g carbohydrate, 4 g fibre, 3 g protein, 0 g fat

polyunsaturated margarine, for greasing
115 g/4 oz ready-to-eat pitted prunes
150 ml/¼ pt water
3 egg whites
⅛ tsp salt
⅛ tsp cream of tartar
15 ml/1 tbsp fructose
1 tsp grated lemon rind

Heat the oven to 180°C/350°F/gas 4 and lightly grease a 750 ml/ 1¼ pt ovenproof serving dish. Put the prunes and water in a saucepan and bring slowly to the boil. Reduce the heat, cover and simmer for 15 minutes. Leave to cool. Purée the prunes and their liquid in a blender.

In a bowl, whisk the egg whites until stiff with the salt and cream of tartar. Whisk in the fructose and lemon rind. Fold the prune purée into the egg whites and transfer to the ovenproof dish. Bake for 25–30 minutes until risen and golden. Serve at once.

MERINGUES

Floating islands ★

Serves 4

Each serving: 126 kcal/530 kJ, 10 g carbohydrate, neg fibre, 8 g protein, 4 g fat →

Tangy lime mousse (*top left*, see page 103); Mango water ice (*top right*, see page 107); Fruit and cheese dessert with Carob sauce (*bottom*, see page 106)

2 eggs, separated
25 g/1 oz fructose
few drops fresh lemon juice
600 ml/1 pt skimmed milk
pared rind of ½ orange
2 tsp cornflour
liquid sweetener, to taste
2 tsp long-thread coconut, toasted
orange peel, cut into julienne strips, to decorate

Put the egg whites in a bowl and whisk until stiff. Whisk in the fructose a spoonful at a time, and then the lemon juice.

Heat the milk in a large shallow pan to simmering point. Using two teaspoons, shape the egg white mixture into sixteen ovals. Drop them into the milk – you may need to do this in two batches – and poach gently for 5 minutes, until firm and puffed. Lift out with a slotted spoon and drain well on kitchen paper towels.

Add the orange rind to the milk. Mix the cornflour and egg yolks together in a bowl and stir in a little hot milk. Pour back into the pan and cook, stirring, until the custard has just thickened. Strain and add liquid sweetener, to taste. Pour the custard on to four individual plates. Arrange four 'islands' on top of each plate of custard and sprinkle with coconut and orange strips.

Variation: Add 50 g/2 oz broken pieces of chocolate to the strained custard. Stir until melted.

Blueberry islands ★ ★ ★

Serves 4 **see photograph, page 84**

Each serving: 69 kcal/291 kJ, 15 g carbohydrate, neg fibre, 2 g protein, 0 g fat

2 egg whites
25 g/1 oz fructose
few drops fresh lemon juice
225 g/8 oz blueberries or other soft fruit
60 ml/4 tbsp low-calorie orange squash
2 tsp arrowroot
150 ml/¼ pt water
orange peel, cut into julienne strips, to decorate

Put the egg whites in a bowl and whisk until stiff. Whisk in the fructose a little at a time, and then the lemon juice.

Bring a large shallow pan of water to simmering point. Add a few drops of lemon juice. Using two teaspoons, shape the egg white into sixteen ovals. Drop them into the simmering water and poach them gently for 5 minutes until firm and puffed – you may have to do this in two batches. Lift out with a slotted spoon and drain well on kitchen paper towels. Combine the blueberries, orange squash, arrowroot and water in a saucepan. Heat gently, stirring all the time, until thickened. Spoon the blueberry sauce on to four individual plates. Arrange the 'islands' on top of the sauce and decorate with strips of orange peel.

JELLIES, CUSTARDS AND MOUSSES

JELLIES

Watermelon and ginger jelly ⊞ ★ ★ ★

Serves 6 **see photograph, page 84**

Each serving: 24 kcal/102 kJ, 5 g carbohydrate, 1 g fibre, 2 g protein, 0 g fat

450 g/1 lb prepared watermelon, puréed
½ tsp ground ginger
25 g/1 oz stem ginger, finely chopped (optional)
15 ml/1 tbsp lemon juice
15 g/½ oz gelatine (or 15 ml/ 1 tbsp)
45 ml/3 tbsp low-calorie lemon squash

Combine the first four ingredients in a bowl. In a small saucepan, dissolve the gelatine in the lemon squash over gentle heat. Remove from the heat and stir in a little of the melon purée. Stir into the watermelon purée in a bowl. Pour the mixture into a 600 ml/1 pt dampened jelly mould and chill until set. Unmould on to a dampened plate.

Note: Any other well-flavoured melon may be used instead of watermelon.

Coconut milk jelly with tropical fruits ★ ★ ★

Serves 4

Each serving: 88 kcal/370 kJ, 15 g carbohydrate, 2 g fibre, 5 g protein, 2 g fat

300 ml/½ pt skimmed milk
2 thin strips lemon rind
15 g/½ oz desiccated coconut
liquid sweetener, to taste
1½ tsp gelatine
30 ml/2 tbsp water
225 g/8 oz prepared tropical fruits (eg. pineapple, mango, kiwi, papaya, banana)

Place the milk and lemon rind in a saucepan and heat very gently for 10 minutes to infuse. Add the coconut and liquid sweetener and leave to cool. →

In a small saucepan, dissolve the gelatine in the water. Remove the lemon rind from the milk and add the milk to the gelatine. Stir well and chill until the mixture has the consistency of unbeaten egg white. Stir well and pour into a 300 ml/½ pt dampened ring mould. Chill until set.

Unmould the jelly on to a flat dish and fill the centre with a mixture of tropical fruits.

Sparkling grape jellies ★ ★

Serves 6 **see photograph, page 95**

Each serving: 87 kcal/364 kJ, 20 g carbohydrate, neg fibre, 3 g protein, neg fat

600 ml/1 pt unsweetened white grape juice
15 g/½ oz gelatine (or 15 ml/1 tbsp)
115 g/4 oz small green or black grapes, halved and pips removed
90 ml/6 tbsp low-fat plain yoghurt, sweetened to taste with fructose or liquid sweetener (optional)

Pour about one quarter of the grape juice into a small saucepan. Sprinkle with the gelatine and dissolve over very gentle heat. Stir in the remaining grape juice and chill until the mixture has the consistency of unbeaten egg white. Stir in the grapes and divide the jelly between four tall glasses. Chill until set.

If wished, top with a little sweetened yoghurt.

Fresh coffee jellies ⊞ ★ ★ ★ ★

Serves 4

Each serving: without cream – 26 kcal/109 kJ, 5 g carbohydrate, 0 g fibre, 2 g protein, 1 g fat

With cream – 62 kcal/260 kJ, 5 g carbohydrate, 0 g fibre, 3 g protein, 4 g fat

450 ml/¾ pt freshly made black coffee
liquid sweetener, to taste
2 tsp gelatine
60 ml/4 tbsp single cream (optional)
4 tsp grated chocolate

Combine the coffee and liquid sweetener, to taste Place 60 ml/4 tbsp of the coffee in a saucepan and sprinkle with gelatine. Heat very gently to dissolve. Add the remaining coffee and transfer to individual glasses. Chill until set.

If wished, pour 15 ml/1 tbsp cream on top of each and sprinkle with grated chocolate just before serving.

Apricot and grape jelly ★ ★ ★

Serves 4

Each serving: 115 kcal/481 kJ, 25 g carbohydrate, 8 g fibre, 5 g protein, 0 g fat

115 g/4 oz dried apricots
300 ml/½ pt unsweetened white grape juice
15 g/½ oz gelatine (or 15 ml/1 tbsp)

To decorate:
grapes, small mint, balm or scented geranium leaves

Wash the apricots and place in a bowl, cover generously with boiling water and leave to soak for at least 12 hours. Drain the apricots, reserving 150 ml/¼ pt of soaking liquid. Purée the apricots and reserved liquid in a food processor or blender. Mix in all but 45 ml/3 tbsp of the grape juice. Place the remaining grape juice in a small saucepan and sprinkle with the gelatine. Dissolve over gentle heat and stir into the apricot mixture. Pour the mixture into a 600 ml/1 pt dampened jelly mould and chill until set.

Unmould and decorate with black or green grapes and the leaves.

Note: This jelly can also be used for spreading on bread, scones, or as a cake filling.

Cranberry and pineapple shimmer ★ ★ ★

Serves 4

Each serving: 61 kcal/256 kJ, 15 g carbohydrate, 1 g fibre, 2 g protein, 0 g fat

300 ml/½ pt pineapple or apple juice (or a mixture of the two)
115 g/4 oz cranberries
1½ tsp gelatine
115 g/4 oz prepared pineapple, finely chopped
liquid sweetener, to taste

Place half the juice in a saucepan. Add the cranberries and simmer gently until they burst and are softened.

In another saucepan, sprinkle the gelatine over the remaining juice and heat gently until dissolved. Mix all the ingredients together and transfer to four individual glasses. Chill until set.

CUSTARDS

Guava custards with toasted coconut ★ ★

Serves 4

see photograph, page 86

Each serving: 113 kcal/476 kJ, 10 g carbohydrate, 4 g fibre, 5 g protein, 6 g fat

285 g/10½ oz can guavas in fruit juice
150 ml/¼ pt skimmed milk
2 eggs
½ tsp vanilla essence
¼ tsp ground ginger
¼ tsp ground nutmeg
60 ml/4 tbsp long-thread coconut, toasted

→

Heat the oven to 170°C/325°F/gas 3.

Purée the contents of the can of guavas in a blender with the skimmed milk, eggs, vanilla essence, ginger and nutmeg. Pour the mixture into four individual ramekin dishes of about 250 ml/8 fl oz capacity.

Place the dishes in a roasting tin. Pour boiling water into the tin to come half-way up the sides of the dishes. Bake for 45 minutes until lightly set. Remove the custards from the tin. Sprinkle each one with a little coconut and serve just warm.

Mango and coconut custards ★ ★

Serves 4

Each serving: 75 kcal/315 kJ, 10 g carbohydrate, 1 g fibre, 2 g protein, 3 g fat

225 ml/8 fl oz thick coconut milk (from a can)
2 tsp cornflour
2 egg yolks
liquid sweetener, to taste (optional)
175 g/6 oz chopped fresh mango
ground nutmeg

Heat the oven to 170°C/325°F/gas 3.

Whisk the coconut milk, cornflour and egg yolks together. Add liquid sweetener to taste, if using. Spoon the prepared mango into four individual ramekin dishes. Pour the custard carefully on top and sprinkle with ground nutmeg.

Place the dishes in a roasting tin. Pour boiling water into the tin to come three-quarters of the way up the sides of the dishes. Bake for about 30 minutes until just firm. Remove from the oven. When cool, chill in the refrigerator.

Variation: Pour the custard mixture into four ramekin dishes and sprinkle with cinnamon. Bake as above. Chill and just before serving, top each one with 50 g/2 oz fresh raspberries.

MOUSSES

Strawberry cheese mousse ★ ★

Serves 10

Each serving: 72 kcal/304 kJ, 5 g carbohydrate, neg fibre, 9 g protein, 1 g fat

411 g/14½ oz can strawberries in fruit juice
225 g/8 oz skimmed-milk soft cheese
15 g/½ oz gelatine (or 15 ml/1 tbsp)
1 quantity Low-calorie topping (see page 111)
fresh strawberries or raspberries, to decorate

Drain the strawberries. Reserve the juice and roughly mash the fruit in a bowl. Stir in the cheese.

Put the gelatine and the reserved fruit juice in a small saucepan and heat gently to dissolve. Stir into the strawberry cheese mixture. Fold the Low-calorie topping into the strawberry mixture. Pour the mixture into a serving dish. Chill until set. Decorate with sliced fresh strawberries or whole raspberries.

Tangy lime mousse

Serves 6

see photograph, page 96

Each serving: 115 kcal/484 kJ, 10 g carbohydrate, neg fibre, 6 g protein, 2 g fat

25 g/1 oz cornflour
450 ml/¾ pt skimmed milk
2 eggs, separated
75 g/3 oz fructose
grated rind and juice of 2 large limes
2 tsp gelatine
fresh lime slices, to decorate

In a bowl, mix the cornflour to a smooth paste with a little of the milk. Beat in the egg yolks. Heat the remaining milk in a saucepan and stir into the egg yolk mixture. Return to the pan and cook, stirring, until the mixture thickens. Remove the pan from the heat and stir in the fructose and lime rind.

In a small saucepan, dissolve the gelatine in the lime juice over gentle heat. Stir into the custard. Whisk the egg whites until stiff and fold into the lime custard. Transfer to a serving dish and chill until required. Decorate with fresh lime slices.

Variation: Use two small lemons or oranges instead of the limes.

Apricot fool

Serves 4

Each serving: 75 kcal/317 kJ, 15 g carbohydrate, 8 g fibre, 3 g protein, 1 g fat

115 g/4 oz dried apricots
115 g/4 oz sheep's milk yoghurt
1 egg white
15 g/½ oz fructose
chopped toasted hazelnuts, to decorate (optional)

Wash the apricots and place in a bowl, cover generously with boiling water and leave to soak for at least 12 hours. Drain and reserve the juice for another recipe. Purée the apricots roughly and stir in the yoghurt.

In another bowl, whisk the egg white until stiff and continue whisking as you sprinkle in the fructose, a little at a time. Fold the egg white into the apricot mixture. Transfer to four individual dishes and chill until required. Decorate with the hazelnuts, if using.

Pumpernickel fool ★ ★ ★

Serves 4 **see photograph, page 62**

Each serving: 134 kcal/563 kJ, 25 g carbohydrate, 3 g fibre, 6 g protein, 1 g fat

350 g/12 oz low-fat plain yoghurt
115 g/4 oz pumpernickel, grated
50 g/2 oz raisins, roughly chopped
grated rind of 1 lemon
liquid sweetener, to taste
1 tsp ground mixed spice
4 strawberries

Mix all the ingredients, except the strawberries, together and spoon into individual dishes. Decorate each one with a whole strawberry.

Note: This dessert will thicken on standing so thin it with a little skimmed milk if necessary.

Chestnut fool ★ ★ ★

Serves 4

Each serving: 171 kcal/719 kJ, 30 g carbohydrate, 4 g fibre, 3 g protein, 4 g fat

225 g/8 oz unsweetened chestnut purée
25 g/1 oz fructose
150 g/5 oz low-fat plain yoghurt
25 g/1 oz chocolate, chopped

In a bowl, beat together the chestnut purée, fructose and yoghurt until smooth. Transfer to four small serving dishes and sprinkle with a little chocolate.

Rhubarb snow ⊞ ★ ★ ★

Serves 4

Each serving: 30 kcal/122 kJ, neg carbohydrate, 2 g fibre, 3 g protein, 0 g fat

225 g/8 oz rhubarb, cut in short lengths
60 ml/4 tbsp orange juice
1½ tsp gelatine
liquid sweetener, to taste
2 egg whites
15 ml/1 tbsp fructose

Put the rhubarb and half the orange juice into a saucepan. Simmer gently until tender. Dissolve the gelatine in the remaining orange juice and stir into the rhubarb. Allow to cool then sweeten to taste with liquid sweetener.

Whisk the egg whites until stiff in a bowl and whisk in the fructose. Fold the rhubarb mixture into the egg whites. Transfer to four individual glasses and chill until set.

YOGHURT AND SOFT CHEESE DESSERTS

Lemon delight with strawberries

★ ★ ★

Serves 4

Each serving: 89 kcal/373 kJ, 10 g carbohydrate, 1 g fibre, 9 g protein, 2 g fat

25 g/1 oz skimmed milk powder
175 g/6 oz curd cheese
grated rind and juice of ½ large lemon
75 ml/5 tbsp low-fat plain yoghurt
liquid sweetener, to taste
ground nutmeg (or cinnamon), to sprinkle
225 g/8 oz fresh strawberries, hulled

In a food processor or blender, combine the milk powder, curd cheese, lemon rind and juice, yoghurt and sweetener and process until smooth.

Transfer to four small ramekin dishes or glasses, sprinkle with nutmeg or cinnamon and top with sliced strawberries.

Real muesli with yoghurt and fresh fruit

★ ★

Serves 4

Each serving: 177 kcal/743 kJ, 25 g carbohydrate, 5 g fibre, 6 g protein, 6 g fat

60 ml/4 tbsp rolled oats, toasted
50 g/2 oz hazelnuts, toasted and chopped
225 g/8 oz low-fat plain yoghurt
1 dessert apple, cored and grated
1 banana, sliced
115 g/4 oz strawberries, hulled and sliced
50 g/2 oz raspberries
liquid sweetener, to taste
skimmed milk, as required

Mix the oats, hazelnuts, yoghurt and apple together. Fold in the fruits and sweeten to taste. If the mixture stands it may need thinning with milk.

Fruit and cheese desserts ★ ★

Serves 8 **see photograph, page 96**

Each serving with Carob sauce: 173 kcal/726 kJ, 20 g carbohydrate, 6 g fibre, 10 g protein, 6 g fat

450 g/1 lb skimmed milk soft cheese
115 g/4 oz sheeps' milk yoghurt
50 g/2 oz almonds, toasted and coarsely chopped
250 g/9 oz dried fruit salad, chopped
½ tsp rosewater
grated rind and juice of 1 tangerine
1 quantity Carob sauce (see below – optional), to serve

In a large bowl, mix all the ingredients together. Use the mixture to fill eight dariole or coeur a la crème moulds. If using the latter, line the moulds with muslin before filling with the mixture. Refrigerate for 2–3 hours.

Unmould on to plates and serve with the carob sauce, if using.

Carob sauce

see photograph, page 96

115 g/4 oz carob bar
60 ml/4 tbsp skimmed milk

Break the carob bar into a saucepan. Add the milk and heat gently, whisking all the time, to make a smooth sauce. Allow to cool before serving.

Chilled apple and orange dessert ★ ★

Serves 6

Each serving: 121 kcal/509 kJ, 20 g carbohydrate, 3 g fibre, 4 g protein, 4 g fat

450 g/1 lb cooking apples, peeled, cored and sliced
grated rind and juice of 1 large orange
25 g/1 oz sultanas
liquid sweetener, to taste
50 g/2 oz coarse oatmeal
50 g/2 oz hazelnuts, roughly chopped
225 g/8 oz low-fat plain yoghurt

Place the apples, orange juice and sultanas in a saucepan and simmer, covered, over very gentle heat for about 15 minutes until soft. Cool, then add liquid sweetener to taste.

Toast the oatmeal and hazelnuts until golden, then leave to go cold.

Mix the yoghurt with the orange rind and further liquid sweetener, to taste.

Layer the three mixtures in one large or six individual dishes, finishing with a layer of yoghurt. Serve lightly chilled.

Coffee and banana dessert ★ ★ ★

Serves 4
Each serving: 111 kcal/466 kJ, 25 g carbohydrate, 3 g fibre, 4 g protein, 1 g fat

2 tsp instant coffee powder
15 ml/1 tbsp boiling water
225 g/8 oz sheep's milk yoghurt
liquid sweetener, to taste
2 large ripe bananas, roughly mashed (reserve a few slices for decoration)

In a bowl, mix the instant coffee powder with the water to dissolve. When cool, beat in the yoghurt and sweeten to taste. Stir in the mashed bananas.

Transfer to four individual glasses and top with slices of banana. Serve at once.

Raspberry cheese delight ★ ★ ★

Serves 4
Each serving: 121 kcal/510 kJ, 5 g carbohydrate, 4 g fibre, 12 g protein, 3 g fat

350 g/12 oz cottage cheese
25 g/1 oz fructose
225 g/8 oz fresh raspberries

Sieve the cottage cheese into a bowl. Mix in the fructose. Purée a scant half of the raspberries and sieve to remove the seeds. Stir into the cheese. Spoon the mixture into a glass serving dish. Top with the remaining raspberries.

Variation: Use any other soft fruit available.

ICES AND SORBETS

Mango water ice ★ ★ ★

Serves 4
see photograph, page 96
Each serving: 105 kcal/441 kJ, 15 g carbohydrate, 1 g fibre, 2 g protein, 0 g fat

350 ml/12 fl oz mango purée (2 medium–large mangoes)
100 ml/4 fl oz soda water
15 ml/1 tbsp fresh lime or lemon juice
2 egg whites
50 g/2 oz fructose
slices of mango or peach, to serve (optional)

→

Mix together the mango purée, soda water and lime or lemon juice in a bowl. In another bowl, whisk the egg whites until stiff, then whisk in the fructose a little at a time. Fold the mango mixture into the egg whites until evenly mixed.

Pour into a rigid container, cover and freeze for about 2 hours or until 'slushy'. Turn out into a large bowl and beat thoroughly – a hand-held electric beater is the most efficient. As soon as the mixture becomes pale and expanded, return to the container and freezer.

Allow the water ice to soften for 30 minutes in the refrigerator before scooping on to plates, or dishes. Decorate with slices of fresh fruit, if wished.

Coconut water ice ⊞ ★ ★ ★

Serves 4

Each serving: 55 kcal/230 kJ, neg carbohydrate, neg fibre, 2 g protein, 0 g fat

225 ml/8 fl oz can thick coconut milk
10 ml/2 tsp fresh lime juice
150 ml/¼ pt soda water
2 egg whites
50 g/2 oz fructose

Stir together the coconut milk, lime juice and soda water. Whisk the egg whites until stiff in a bowl. Whisk in the fructose a little at a time. Fold the coconut mixture into the egg whites.

Transfer to a rigid container, cover and freeze for about 2 hours or until 'slushy'. Turn out into a large bowl and beat well. Return to the container and freeze until required.

Allow to soften for 30 minutes in the refrigerator before serving. Serve in scoops.

Note: If wished, serve with a decoration of thinly sliced pineapple and a cherry or strawberry for colour.

Rhubarb and strawberry ice ⊞ ★ ★ ★

Serves 4

Each serving: 16 kcal/69 kJ, 5 g carbohydrate, 2 g fibre, 2 g protein, 0 g fat

175 g/6 oz prepared rhubarb, cut in 2.5 cm/1 inch lengths
15 ml/1 tbsp water
125 g/4 oz ripe strawberries, hulled
1 tsp gelatine
45 ml/3 tbsp low-calorie orange squash
liquid sweetener, to taste
4 strawberries, to decorate

Put the rhubarb and water in a saucepan and simmer until just tender. Remove from the heat. Roughly crush the strawberries and add to the rhubarb. Dissolve the gelatine in the orange squash and stir into the fruit. Leave to go cold. Add liquid sweetener to taste.

Transfer the mixture to a rigid container. Cover and freeze for about 2 hours or until 'slushy'. Turn the mixture out into a large bowl and beat well. Return to the container and freeze until required.

Allow to soften to room temperature and roughly crush. Transfer to glasses and serve topped with a strawberry.

Pear sorbet ⊞ ★ ★ ★

Serves 4

Each serving: 54 kcal/228 kJ, 10 g carbohydrate, 2 g fibre, 0 g protein, 0 g fat

411 g/14½ oz can pears in fruit juice
1 tsp gelatine
45 ml/3 tbsp low-calorie lemon and lime squash
1 egg white

Purée the pears with their juice in a blender. Dissolve the gelatine in the fruit squash over gentle heat. Remove from the heat and add the pear purée.

When cold pour the mixture into a rigid container. Cover and freeze for about 2 hours or until the mixture is 'slushy'. Turn the mixture out into a large bowl. Stiffly whisk the egg white and fold into the pear mixture. Return to the container and freeze until required.

Allow to soften in the refrigerator for 30 minutes before serving.

Watermelon granita ⊞ ★ ★ ★

Serves 4

Each serving: 35 kcal/147 kJ, 10 g carbohydrate, 1 g fibre, 1 g protein, 0 g fat

450 ml/¾ pt watermelon purée (made from about 450–600 g/1–1¼ lb melon)
1½ tsp cornflour
15 ml/1 tbsp fresh lime juice
liquid sweetener, to taste

Mix together about one-quarter of the melon purée with the cornflour and lime juice. Cook, stirring until thickened. Remove from the heat and stir in the remaining melon purée. Cool, then add liquid sweetener to taste.

Freeze in a rigid container for about 2 hours until 'slushy'. Spoon into individual glasses and serve at once.

Note: The granita can also be stored in the freezer. Allow it to soften in the refrigerator to a 'slushy' consistency before serving.

FILLINGS AND TOPPINGS

Apricot cheese filling ★ ★ ★

Sufficient to fill and top a 20 cm/8 inch cake
Total recipe: 278 kcal/1168 kJ, 45 g carbohydrate, 24 g fibre, 18 g protein, 4 g fat

115 g/4 oz dried apricots, washed and soaked overnight
115 g/4 oz low-fat soft cheese
liquid sweetener, to taste

Just cover the apricots with water in a saucepan and bring to the boil. Cover and simmer for about 25 minutes until soft. Drain, reserving the juice for another dish. Purée the apricots in a bowl. Cover and put in the refrigerator to chill. Fold in the soft cheese and add liquid sweetener to taste.

Pastry cream ★ ★

Makes about 300 ml/½ pt
Total recipe: 376 kcal/1579 kJ, 55 g carbohydrate, 1 g fibre, 18 g protein, 10 g fat

2 egg yolks
30 ml/2 tbsp cornflour
15 ml/1 tbsp plain flour
350 ml/13 fl oz skimmed milk
1 vanilla pod (or a few drops vanilla essence)
liquid sweetener, to taste

Put the egg yolks in a bowl and whisk until pale. Beat in the cornflour and flour and sufficient milk to make a smooth paste.

Heat the remaining milk in a saucepan with the vanilla pod to just below boiling point. Remove from the heat and leave to infuse for 5 minutes. Stir the milk into the egg yolk mixture and return to the pan. Cook, stirring all the time, until thickened.

Strain and add liquid sweetener to taste. Cover and chill until required. Use as a filling or spread. It will keep in the refrigerator for two to three days, covered.

Note: If using vanilla essence, add with the liquid sweetener.

Variations
Orange or lemon – omit the vanilla pod; use a few strips of pared orange or lemon rind.

Bay or rosemary – omit the vanilla pod; use a fresh bay leaf or sprig of fresh rosemary.
Almond – omit the vanilla pod; add a few drops of almond essence.
Chocolate – add 50 g/2 oz grated chocolate, stir until melted.

Date and banana spread ★ ★ ★

Makes 350 g/12 oz
Total recipe: 517 kcal/2170 kJ, 110 g carbohydrate, 13 g fibre, 12 g protein, 5 g fat

115 g/4 oz stoned dates
1 banana
½ quantity Pastry cream (see opposite)

Mince or purée the dates in a food processor or blender. Mash the banana and beat all the ingredients together until evenly combined.

Use at once as bananas discolour quite soon.

Note: Serve on bread or as a filling for a sandwich cake.

Almond paste ★

Makes about 175 g/6 oz
Total recipe: 616 kcal/2588 kJ, 5 g carbohydrate, 14 g fibre, 19 g protein, 58 g fat

115 g/4 oz ground almonds
25 g/1 oz fructose
1 egg yolk
1 tsp lemon juice
¼ tsp almond essence

Mix the ground almonds and fructose in a bowl. Add the remaining ingredients and work together to make a firm paste.

Use as an icing or filling.

Note: The paste will store in the refrigerator for up to one week, well wrapped.

Low-calorie topping ★ ★ ★

Makes about 600 ml/1 pt
Total recipe: 268 kcal/1126 kJ, 20 g carbohydrate, 0 g fibre, 27 g protein, 0 g fat

1½ tsp gelatine
150 ml/¼ pt iced water
40 g/1½ oz skimmed milk powder
30 ml/2 tbsp fructose
¼ tsp vanilla essence

→

In a small saucepan, dissolve the gelatine in about one-quarter of the water over a gentle heat. Leave to cool.

Whisk together the remaining water and milk powder using a hand-held electric whisk for about 2 minutes until frothy and increased in volume. Slowly whisk in the gelatine, fructose and vanilla and continue whisking until soft peaks form. Use immediately.

Note: Do not refrigerate this topping because it will set to a foam jelly.

Variation

Coffee – add 30 ml/2 tbsp fructose and 2 tsp instant coffee dissolved in 30 ml/2 tbsp hot water.

Lemon, orange or lime – omit the vanilla essence and add 1–2 tsp grated lemon, lime or orange rind. You may wish to increase the amount of sweetening, to taste.

Pouring custard ☒ ☒

Makes about 300 ml/½ pt **see photograph, page 73**

Total recipe: 185 kcal/779 kJ, 25 g carbohydrate, 0 g fibre, 13 g protein, 5 g fat

300 ml/½ pt skimmed milk
1 egg yolk
2 tsp cornflour
few drops vanilla essence
liquid sweetener, to taste

Place most of the milk in a saucepan and bring to just below boiling point.

In a bowl, combine the remaining milk with the egg yolk and cornflour and blend to a smooth paste. Pour the hot milk over the egg mixture, stir well and return to the saucepan. Heat gently, stirring constantly, until the mixture thickens. Remove from the heat and stir in the vanilla essence and liquid sweetener. Serve immediately.

'SWEETS'

Orange coconut nuggets ★

Makes 18

Each nugget: 105 kcal/443 kJ, 10 g carbohydrate, 1 g fibre, 1 g protein, 6 g fat

100 g/3½ oz polyunsaturated margarine, plus extra for greasing
65 g/2½ oz fructose
25 g/1 oz desiccated coconut
1 tsp grated orange rind
15 ml/1 tbsp orange juice
175 g/6 oz self-raising flour
45 ml/3 tbsp long-thread or desiccated coconut, to decorate

Heat the oven to 190°C/375°F/gas 5 and lightly grease a baking sheet. Put the margarine and fructose in a bowl and cream until light and fluffy. Stir in the coconut, orange rind and juice and work in the flour. Drop spoonfuls of the mixture on to the baking sheet. Sprinkle each one with a little coconut and press gently. Bake for about 15 minutes until golden. Cool on a wire tray.

Prune and pecan bites ★ ★

Makes 12

Each one: 35 kcal/148 kJ, 5 g carbohydrate, 2 g fibre, 1 g protein, 2 g fat

115 g/4 oz ready-to-eat prunes, soaked for 5 minutes in boiling water
50 g/2 oz shelled pecan nuts (or walnuts)

Place the prunes and pecans in a grinder or food processor until finely chopped. Divide the mixture into twelve pieces and form each into a small ball. Leave on greaseproof paper to dry out for a few hours. Serve in petits fours cases.

Fresh stuffed figs ★ ★

Serves 4

Each serving: 84 kcal/355 kJ, 10 g carbohydrate, 1 g fibre, 5 g protein, 4 g fat

8 fresh figs, washed
115 g/4 oz skimmed-milk soft cheese
finely grated rind of 2 tangerines
25 g/1 oz pistachio nuts, chopped
25 g/1 oz raisins, chopped
liquid sweetener, to taste

→

Cut the stalks off the figs. Without cutting right through the fruit, make three cuts in each fig so that it opens out into six petals. Combine the remaining ingredients and divide between the figs. Draw up the 'petals' around the filling. Arrange on individual serving plates.

Coconut bars

Makes 4
Each bar: 121 kcal/510 kJ, 10 g carbohydrate, 4 g fibre, 2 g protein, 9 g fat

40 g/1½ oz desiccated coconut
20 g/¾ oz unsalted cashew nuts or peanuts
50 g/2 oz raisins
15 g/½ oz fresh pineapple

Heat the oven to 200°C/400°F/gas 6.

Put the coconut and cashew nuts on a non-stick baking sheet and toast in the oven for about 10 minutes, or until golden brown.

Place all ingredients in a grinder or food processor and work the mixture until it holds together well. Roll out between two sheets of non-stick paper to a rectangle 15 × 10 cm/6 × 4 inches. Cut into four bars. Leave overnight to dry out.

Date bars

Makes 12
Each bar: 132 kcal/554 kJ, 15 g carbohydrate, 2 g fibre, 4 g protein, 6 g fat

100 g/3½ oz polyunsaturated margarine, plus extra for greasing
50 g/2 oz fructose
150 g/5 oz stoned dates, finely chopped
75 g/3 oz self-raising flour
25 g/1 oz rolled oats
pinch of salt

Heat the oven to 180°C/350°F/gas 4 and lightly grease a 20 cm/8 inch shallow square tin. Put the margarine and fructose in a bowl and cream together until pale and fluffy. Stir in the remaining ingredients. Press the mixture into the tin. Bake for about 30 minutes until golden. Allow to cool in the tin, then cut into bars.

FESTIVE DESSERTS

Christmas pudding

Makes 2 puddings (550 g/1¼ lb, each pudding serves 4)
Each serving: 301 kcal/1264 kJ, 40 g carbohydrate, 7 g fibre, 7 g protein, 15 g fat

115 g/4 oz wholemeal flour
1 tsp baking powder
50 g/2 oz wholemeal breadcrumbs
50 g/2 oz ground almonds
50 g/2 oz polyunsaturated margarine, plus extra for greasing
1 large carrot, finely grated
3 eggs
550 g/1¼ lb Spiced mincemeat (see page 116)

Lightly grease two 750 ml/1¼ pt pudding basins. Combine all the ingredients in a bowl and beat well until evenly mixed. Divide the mixture between the pudding basins. Cover each basin with a greased round of foil with a central pleat to allow for expansion. Tie securely with string. Steam or, alternatively, place the pudding basins in two large saucepans; pour in boiling water to come half-way up the sides of the basins, cover with a lid and simmer for 2 hours. Add more boiling water, if necessary. Remove the basins from the pans and leave to go cold.

Remove the puddings from the basins and wrap well in greaseproof paper and foil. Store in the refrigerator or, if keeping for more than two days, freeze. To reheat, unwrap the puddings, return to the pudding basins and steam or boil for 1 hour. Serve with Pouring custard (see page 112).

Mince pies

Makes 18
Each pie: 108 kcal/455 kJ, 15 g carbohydrate, 2 g fibre, 2 g protein, 6 g fat

1 quantity Basic wholemeal pastry (see page 43)
275 g/10 oz Spiced mincemeat (see page 116)

Heat the oven to 200°C/400°F/gas 6. Roll out the pastry on a lightly floured surface and stamp out rounds to fit eighteen patty tins. Fill each one with the mincemeat.

Reroll the pastry trimmings and stamp out eighteen lids. Dampen the edges of the pastry and seal each pie carefully. Using a sharp knife, make a small slit in each pie. Bake for 20 minutes. Serve warm or cold.

Spiced mincemeat ★

Makes about 1.5 kg/3½ lb

Total recipe: 3013 kcal/12655 kJ, 555 g carbohydrate, 75 g fibre, 24 g protein, 92 g fat

225 g/8 oz cooking apples, peeled, cored and grated
grated rind and juice of 1 lemon
grated rind and juice of 1 orange
50 g/2 oz polyunsaturated margarine
225 g/8 oz currants
225 g/8 oz sultanas
225 g/8 oz raisins
115 g/4 oz dried figs, chopped
300 ml/½ pt apple juice
½ tsp ground cinnamon
½ tsp ground nutmeg
½ tsp ground mixed spice
½ tsp ground mace
¼ tsp ground cloves
125 g/4 oz shelled walnuts, chopped

Place all the ingredients except the walnuts in a large saucepan and bring to the boil. Reduce the heat, cover the pan and simmer, stirring occasionally, for 1 hour.

Allow the mincemeat to cool then stir in the walnuts. Spoon into jars or rigid plastic containers, cover and store in the refrigerator. It will keep in the refrigerator for up to one week.

ACKNOWLEDGMENTS

I am very grateful to Anne Hildyard for her help with the recipes, to Louise Pickford for assisting with the food photography, and to Nova Pilbeam for typing the recipes.

Jane Suthering *1986*

I should like to thank the following for their help and advice: Pat Butler, Jackie Edington, Joanna Lousley, Jill Metcalfe (from the British Diabetic Association), Margaret Thorogood and David Yeates.

Sue Lousley *1986*

The publishers would like to thank Peter Myers and his assistant, Neil Mersh, for the photography, and Penny Markham for the styling. The food was prepared for photography by Jane Suthering.

INDEX

Page numbers in *italic* refer to the illustrations

Other books for diabetics in the Positive Health Guide series:

DIABETES: A PRACTICAL NEW GUIDE TO HEALTHY LIVING
Dr James Anderson
Written especially for those with newly diagnosed diabetes, this book is packed with information on diet, insulin, exercise, and coping with everyday life – the best help for diabetics is self-help, and this book provides it.

THE DIABETICS' DIET BOOK
Dr Jim Mann and the Oxford Dietetic Group
The first book to explain how a high-carbohydrate and fibre diet can lead to better control of diabetes, including over 140 mouthwatering recipes which the whole family will enjoy.

THE DIABETICS' COOKBOOK
Roberta Longstaff, SRD, and Dr Jim Mann
The sequel to the bestselling *The Diabetics' Diet Book*, this book not only contains wholesome everyday meals, but also exciting dishes for dinner and drinks parties, children's meals, and food for festive occasions.

THE DIABETICS' GET FIT BOOK
Jacki Winter and Dr Barbara Boucher
At last – a complete home workout routine written by an insulin dependent diabetic specially for diabetics. Here's how to get fit and stay fit whatever your age and ability.

THE HEALTHY HEART DIET BOOK
Enjoy delicious low-fat, high-fibre recipes
Roberta Longstaff, SRD, and Dr Jim Mann

BEAT HEART DISEASE
A cardiologist explains how you can help your heart and enjoy a healthier life
Prof Risteard Mulcahy

THE SALT-FREE DIET BOOK
An appetizing way to help reduce high blood pressure
Dr Graham MacGregor

CARING FOR AN ELDERLY RELATIVE
A guide to home care
Dr Keith Thompson

THE VEGETARIAN'S HEALTHY DIET BOOK
150 nutritious recipes
Colin Spencer
Introduction by Dr Tom Sanders

COOKING FOR KIDS THE HEALTHY WAY
Wholesome recipes with child appeal
Joanna Pay, SRD

EYES: THEIR PROBLEMS AND TREATMENTS
Michael Glasspool, FRCS

KEEPING BABIES AND CHILDREN HEALTHY
A parents' practical handbook to common ailments
Dr Bernard Valman

THE HYPERACTIVE CHILD
A parents' guide
Dr Eric Taylor

CHILDREN'S PROBLEMS
A parents' guide to understanding and tackling them
Dr Bryan Lask